WHAT IF I'M WRONG?

WHAT IF I'M WRONG?

NAVIGATING THE WAVES OF FEAR AND FAILURE

HEATHER THOMPSON DAY

W PUBLISHING GROUP

AN IMPRINT OF THOMAS NELSON

What If I'm Wrong?

Published in Nashville, Tennessee, by W Publishing, an imprint of Thomas Nelson.

Author represented by MacGregor and Luedeke Literary agency.

Thomas Nelson titles may be purchased in bulk for educational, business, fundraising, or sales promotional use. For information, please email SpecialMarkets@ThomasNelson.com.

ISBN 978-1-4003-4160-3 (audiobook)
ISBN 978-1-4003-4159-7 (ePub)
ISBN 978-1-4003-4157-3 (TP)

Library of Congress Control Number: 2024949151

Printed in the United States of America
25 26 27 28 29 LBC 5 4 3 2 1

I dedicate this book to my father, Joel James Jefferson Thompson. I've never known a person of more passion—or more faith.

CONTENTS

CONTENTS

CHAPTER 1

WHAT IF I'M WRONG?

I'M DROWNING.

I wrote these words in my prayer journal. No context. No amen. Not so much a prayer as a cry for help. Two words that felt like a metaphor for the chaos that was devouring my hopes, dreams, and vision for my future. Passion should come with caution signals. It's a strong wave over all who dare to greet it. The same water that raises you up can sweep you beneath its current.

I learned about passion from my father. His lessons have haunted me my entire life. There is a fine line between faith and delusion. I can't always tell which side of it my dad was on. I've never known anyone who trusted God more fully. Dad was diagnosed with Alzheimer's when I was twenty-five. He never once complained. But I've done enough complaining for both of us. My nana, who raised ten children, was a musician. She played the organ in church while my dad was growing up. He didn't have a present father in his life. And he never talked like this was a problem.

"When I was little, probably six or seven, I asked God to be my dad," my father used to tell me. "And I know without a doubt that God answered that request."

When Dad was seventeen, he went into show business. He'd play his guitar outside the office of whatever record label executive he hoped would sign him. Sometimes he was kicked out, other times he was welcomed. He got a part in his first Broadway show by memorizing the dance routine in one of the numbers, then running onto the stage from the audience and performing it beside the cast. The bouncer kicked him out, but not before a producer gave him his card. My dad believed that risk was a small price to pay for reward. He also believed that God placed gifts within humanity and that using them honored God.

I know what it feels like to have your dreams bury you beneath them. That's why I was drowning. I had forgotten the rules of adulthood. I jumped headfirst into the waves of passion, thinking it would bring me safely to my purpose. But passion does nothing safely. It's a harrowing front stroke into deep water with a strong current. It offers only risk, pain, and reward. Stay on the shore if you want safety. This is a common misconception, that our passions can be pursued from a safe distance. That we can give in to hope without eventually losing it.

Biblically speaking, the word *passion* literally means "to suffer."[1] It is about doing what we feel called to do, even though it brings us great suffering. The word finds its root in the Latin word *passiō* and the Greek word *pathos*. Both communicate suffering. That is why they called it "the passion of

Christ." I don't know if it is even considered passion until the suffering starts.

For Dad, his dream was to be an actor on Broadway. He starred in shows like *Jesus Christ Superstar* and *Hair*. One day, however, he felt a deeply supernatural call to leave New York City and pursue ministry. He packed everything up, including my mom and my sister (this was before I was born) and moved to a small Midwestern town near Lake Michigan, where he would spend the rest of his life devoted to that call. He studied theology. He created a radio program called *Kids Are Christians Too!* from our basement. He wrote songs and sermons. He created entire musicals all on old carpet under a small window that brought two tiny shafts of light.

Who knows what could have happened for him career-wise had he stayed in New York? He traded Broadway stages and lights for an old blue van we all piled in. We had family worship by the lake. Instead of Broadway, the wind and waves applauded him. I was always as mesmerized by my dad as I was by the water. In both, I hoped to see myself. One day he was on the late show with Johnny Carson, and the next day he became the man I saw tiptoeing down into the basement to groan before the Lord. I am not exaggerating when I tell you my dad is one of the most talented people you've ever heard sing. That dichotomy has always struck me. That there can be incredibly gifted people who are faithful with the seeds God has given them and yet God doesn't bless them in a way that at least American Christianity would deem "blessed and highly favored."

The hand of God over your life is not always visible by financial measure or popularity. In fact, I would go as far as to say that there is no correlation to financial prosperity and spiritual anointing. Consumerism is not the marker of God's presence. The prophets of Israel lived lives that can attest to this. I used to think there was a correlation between the size of the crowd and the size of the gifting. I know now that this is not true. There are successful people in every industry who have made it by their own strength, not God's. And there are people I have known personally without crowds or financial resources, and the Spirit of God is heavy upon them. It is difficult to understand the ways of heaven while still on earth. It is hard to fathom the ways of a God who causes the sun to shine on both the righteous and the wicked. It doesn't seem fair to me. And God doesn't seem to mind. I have had to stop trying to understand it. But I have learned to trust God anyway.

I was on a run the other day, and a thought dropped into my head that brought me to tears mid-mile. *I don't have to perceive that God is being good to me in order to partake in God's goodness. And God doesn't have to bless me in order to partake in blessing someone else.* Because of this ever-present invitation of heaven toward humanity to bring both goodness and blessing to others despite what we feel we haven't received, experiencing the goodness of God and the blessings of God are available to us in every season. That is a gift that belongs only to the righteous. The wicked could never conceive of it.

Dad was an example to me of bringing the goodness and blessing of God into the world despite your circumstances. He was a sincerely faithful Christian. He didn't talk about God as much as he talked with God, and he talked about God a lot. Joel Thompson gave up his literal dream to follow the call of God. And he believed, as he stepped outside the boat, that God would honor that leap.

Every weekend my family crammed into the van. We traveled to wherever Dad was speaking. My favorite place to sit during one of his programs was under the sound booth. My mom became an audio engineer on weekends. She ran special effects and knew when to switch from one audio to the next. That was her contribution. My contribution was to sleep under the sound booth. My mom was a wife and mother who had a full-time job outside of the house that supported our family insurance, and now she became an audio engineer. She gave everything for my dad's calling. We all did.

I don't think my mom ever doubted my dad's choice to give everything to his passion. At least not until the Alzheimer's. Watching the person you love slowly forget everything they always knew changes what you remember. All our happy memories have a twinge of sadness now. When I think about who my dad was to us, I have a parallel image in my mind of who the disease has made him become, and it sets fire to the background of a lot of my memories. He didn't know when he taught me to pray how those prayers would one day consume me. That I would pace my block for weeks and years begging God to reveal his goodness toward my family in some way that made my dad's Alzheimer's feel justified. Like God had made an even trade. I needed redemption for the broken pieces. I have yet to get it.

I wanted God to prove to me that he remembered everything my dad was forgetting. That God would honor our pain somehow. He would bless all those years of effort. My faith, and in turn the faith I remember my dad having, is much more complicated for me now. Should we have trusted Dad as much as we did? Should Dad have trusted God as much as he did? Scripture says not to worry about tomorrow, and to be honest, there are days when I wish we all had worried more.

That worry has informed a lot of our choices. My sister is a nurse practitioner who works in pediatrics. I don't remember her wanting to be anything else even as a kid. She always wanted to deliver babies. That and make money. She encouraged her husband to go back to school for a career transition later in life. He's a lawyer now. There are few things more important to my sister than financial resources. Not because she's greedy but because she values stability. When you grow up without a lot of financial stability, you dream of one day securing it. I can remember one Saturday night nearly a dozen years ago when my sister, brother, and I all knelt down in my parents' living room while they were gone. We were all so poor we didn't have a pot to piss in.

"Lord, please give us stability," we said one by one. We had watched our parents give up everything financially and emotionally to pursue my dad's ministry. After all, it was his passion. And with passion comes suffering. Today, my sister finds stability in paychecks. I find it in early morning prayers. But essentially, we are both doing the same thing. We are trying to secure safety.

I had a PhD by thirty-one. At my core, I was chasing stability. And I was trying to earn it with degrees. I was distancing myself from what I saw my dad do: Go all in on his passion with no fail-safe. Trust God with no backup plan. My dad didn't mind rejection or disappointment. It didn't faze him.

"Sometimes you sink, and sometimes you swim," he'd say. Dad didn't avoid the possibility of failure.

I'd spend the rest of my life doing anything I could to avoid it. I didn't want to be differentiated from my dad until I found out he had Alzheimer's. I think I still believed in his dreams up until I found out he'd gotten sick. This diagnosis would be the undertow that would suck me away from the transactional God I had believed in. Good people reap blessings, bad people reap curses. My dad had been shorted on his transaction. He knew the God who had the sun shine on both the righteous and the wicked. It didn't feel fair. And there is no use in trying to understand it. God is complex and so is theology.

Isn't that how it goes for most of us? We spend our entire lives trying to be exactly like our parents or totally opposite of them. I think for me it's been both. I want to be everything like my father in devotion but totally unlike him in financial stability. I want to be rich and righteous. I'm using an exaggeration to make a point that I think a lot of us are seeking a God who holds to the transaction. Who makes the sun shine a bit brighter and hotter on those of us who have been "good." Who allows us to be rich and righteous. I'd spend years trying to earn them both. If my dad was still the dad I knew growing up, he would say that both are out of your control and that, unlike money, righteousness can't be earned.

"God is going to let me pour out," he'd say to my mom and me even after the Alzheimer's diagnosis. He meant pour out in his ministry. He started taking notes on all the changes he was experiencing mentally. I almost think he enjoyed it. He would give God glory through his suffering. He would prove that God still did miracles. He had a recurring dream in the beginning of his diagnosis that he and I were on a TV show together and he was talking to people about Alzheimer's. He started writing a book. It was called *Alzheimer's from the Inside Out.* He would never be able to finish it. It never occurred to my dad that this new season of his life wouldn't bear fruit.

"God will take care of me," he would say.

And if I am honest, there have been many days when I feel like God didn't.

If you've ever loved someone with Alzheimer's, you know that you essentially learn to love a new person. My dad as I knew him growing up has evaporated. But there is a new man in his place whom I've learned to love the same. My dad is the reason I started going to therapy.

"What scares you the most," my therapist asked, "about losing your dad?" It was the first time anyone had ever directly asked me such a personal question. My mom barely said the word *Alzheimer's.* We all just pretended it wasn't happening.

"All of it," I told her, sobbing. "I don't know if I'll still be me without him. So much of who I am is because of him," I cried.

"Do you know, when people die, you don't lose what they've given you?" she asked me sincerely. "All the pillars your dad built in your life stay, even when he is gone."

There was something incredibly comforting about this. That I would still be me without him. That I wouldn't lose the lessons even if I lost the teacher. That life is about building pillars that hold others up long after we are gone.

I intentionally looked for a therapist who wasn't a Christian. I have sound Christian counsel in my life. I have people who will spiritualize every event. I have mentors of great faith who see that which is in the distance as if it is up close. So when looking for a therapist, I wanted the opposite of that. Losing my dad had me grappling with a new understanding of God. I was drowning. And I didn't understand how God operated anymore. I couldn't quantify his work without his keeping up his end of the transaction. It felt like God had discarded my dad, a man who trusted him wholly. I didn't know if I could rely on this God. A God who lets some dreams get lost at sea. A God who didn't make me rich or all that righteous. A God who let my spiritual hero get Alzheimer's. I wanted a therapist who wasn't Christian because I wanted someone to tell me the cold, hard truth if I was more delusional than faithful. If nihilism was where this bus stopped, I wanted to face it head-on. I wanted someone who would tell me if the dreams I grew up with were inspired or just insanity. Sometimes you need someone outside the bubble to peer into it and tell you if it's madness.

"Even if none of it is real," she said, looking at me kindly, "how has it hurt you? Would you say your life looks better because of your faith, or worse?" I thought a non-Christian would be more antagonistic. I needed the truth, not rational empathy.

"If God hasn't called me to these things, then I have spent my entire life wrestling, and praying, and suffering for no reason," I told her. "Don't you see? I could be a crazy person," I said, sincerely concerned all this God, purpose, passion stuff was driving me mad.

"Of all the people who know you best and love you, is there a single one who thinks you're crazy?" she asked.

"No . . ." I said, frustrated. I needed a smoking gun.

"So, let's say all this time you have been wrong about what you thought God called you to," she said.

That's right, lady. Give it to me straight, I thought. *Burst this bubble. Let me drown.*

"I wouldn't assign judgment to it. Your belief in what you feel called to has given you a deep sense of purpose. Would you be where you are today without it? Your life, objectively, seems pretty meaningful."

What about you? If you hadn't lived your life thinking God had called you to "this," whatever "this" is, how would your life look different? Has your passion for that thing given you a deep sense of purpose? How have all these years of work made your life more meaningful? Take it from my non-Christian therapist. If you feel you've been fruitlessly fishing for purpose, what if your time on the water has made you a better version of yourself? What if the same waves that break us, form us? Is it possible that your passion, while painful, has also made you beautiful?

I'd be willing to bet that there is fruit on the branches of your life. Maybe it isn't money or power. Maybe you don't feel important. But what if those types of fruit aren't the fruit of heaven anyway? I think that while I was praying to be rich and righteous, my dad was praying to serve humbly and with integrity. God honored those prayers. And God will honor yours.

I texted my mom as I was writing this. It brought up a lot of feelings, and I needed to say it to someone who would recognize the sting.

"I watched Dad devote his entire life to ministry, and a pain point for me is knowing he has nothing to show for it," I wrote.

"You say Dad has nothing to show for it?" she texted me back fifty-nine minutes later, though my read receipt said she had seen it immediately. She spent fifty-nine minutes thinking about what I had said. Fifty-nine minutes to say what she would respond with next.

"He has you to show for it. If you are continuing his passion, then it doesn't really end with him, does it? It just keeps going, from generation to generation. Don't say Dad has nothing to show for it. He has you to show for it. Heather, what if you're wrong?"

It's a question I hope you will ask yourself at least once throughout our time together. It's a question I haven't stopped asking myself since my mother sent that text message. It's easy for me, on a bad day, to look at my life and wonder if I'll ever have anything to show for it. Maybe I didn't inherit my father's faithfulness. Maybe I need security and safety more than I need to dream. I often worry that all of this passion will eventually drown me. But lately, I have started to wonder,

What if I'm wrong?

Those who hope in the LORD will renew their strength. They will soar on wings like eagles; they will run and not grow weary, they will walk and not be faint.

Isaiah 40:31

DIVE DEEPER

1. What was your parents' faith like?
2. Where do you find your stability?
3. What are you passionate about?

CHAPTER 2

DEEP WATER

FOUR YEARS AGO, MY MENTOR, JOSÉ ROJAS, called me. I was packing up my house in Denver to move back to Michigan. I needed some time to be closer to my parents as my dad's Alzheimer's worsened. José prays for me regularly, and now and then he'll call me when he feels the Lord has given him a word for my life. He had a word, and I had an ear.

"The Lord is taking you to deeper water," he said. "You've been near the shore. But he is going to take you deeper. Be unafraid."

We talked a bit, but I never asked him what "deep water" was symbolic of. So, when he said that I was going into deep water, I assumed I knew what that meant. I did not. Which is probably why I have sat down to share everything I now know with you. Because every swimmer will eventually come into deep water. From the time I hung up the phone with José that day, my life ventured into the sea.

Did you know that water often represents chaos in the Bible?[1] A fitting depiction for how many of us may find our lives. Engulfed in water. Swirling in confusion and disorder. A realm with no rules or fair treatment. In Genesis, we find ourselves waist-deep in the creation story; not even one sentence in, we are surrounded by water.

Genesis 1:1–2 reads, "In the beginning God created the heavens and the earth. Now the earth was formless and empty, darkness was over the surface of the deep, and the Spirit of God was hovering over the waters."

Other versions, like the Living Bible (TLB), will relay this passage a bit differently. It says, "The earth was a shapeless, chaotic mass." So, in Genesis, we see God as Creator, creating light where there was darkness. And we learn something right there in the first few lines of Scripture that I hope to remind you of throughout our time together: that God has, since the very beginning, had the power to bring order to chaos. In fact, in Genesis 2:10 we get another theme of water that is the opposite side of chaos. It says in the Christian Standard Bible that "a river went out from Eden to water the garden."

In Genesis 1 and 2 we see that God is never threatened by the water that threatens us; in fact, the rivers and water that come from God, and not our chaotic world, can give and bring life to the entire earth.

On day one of creation God had the power to separate the light from the darkness, and on day two of creation God separated the water above from the water below. On day three God divided the water from the land. For three days God was making the earth habitable by controlling the water. God, since the very beginning in Genesis, was "passionate" about bringing order to the chaos of our little world (Genesis 1). Creation and new creation. We see this theme over and over in Scripture. Deep water often represents deep trouble, but Christ is the water of eternal life. It would have been nice if José had mentioned this before hanging up.

My life was going well. It was July. Surely winter wouldn't come in summer. Surely the chaos waters wouldn't pull me beneath them. I had just come off a massive high of seeing God directly answer my prayer by allowing me to move back to Michigan, which would bring me closer to my dad. I had a book that was a Christian bestseller. I was in the process of writing another book. I was living a writer's dream. The water of life was a river flowing out of me. No one had yet told me that passion meant suffering. If this was the shore, baby, pull me out to sea! Drop me like a cannonball. I thought deep water meant even richer blessings. Plot twist: it didn't.

Almost since my feet stepped onto Michigan dirt, my life got increasingly more complicated. Ancient Israel couldn't have prepared me for the obstacles that were going to crash into my life like a wave. I put five offers on houses I loved that all fell through. If you read my husband Seth's and my book *I'll See You Tomorrow*, you know we lived for six months as a family of five in my parents' basement before we finally got our home. My husband struggled to find a job in a small town with limited opportunities. He was offered six jobs in twelve months, but none of them would let us live near my dad, and I needed this time with him. You can imagine what this tension did to our marriage. Seth needed to go left, but my heart could only turn right. He had to choose between his career and my commitment to be by the side of my ailing father. And in so many different ways, it didn't *feel* like God was rewarding him for this sacrificial posture. That's the truth about adulthood math: You don't always get what you give.

I began therapy almost immediately after moving back to Michigan. I started processing losing my dad as I had always known him. I would sit in my therapist's Zoom room while in my campus office where I was an associate professor and dig my nails into my thigh. In therapy I discovered that I had used things like work and achievements to avoid my grief. I was thirty-three years old and just now discovering that I had been living fairly numb. I didn't feel like I had the time to do the emotional labor of unpacking everything that made me feel bad, so I chose instead to throw myself into projects and guiding students so I wouldn't feel anything.

Suffering is time-consuming, and therapy was a rabbit hole that led me into much self-discovery. As I shared with my therapist about my grief, it opened up something in me. I couldn't turn off my feelings as well anymore. I started to feel nervous before teaching my classes. I had been teaching for over a decade, but as I allowed my mind to be present in my own body, I started realizing that I wasn't a machine. I was a person, and I was tired.

My exhaustion revealed itself to me one day in a meeting. Someone I worked with said something that really bothered me. Their comment struck me as insensitive to a particular group of students. I noticed as I was responding that my volume was rising, and my heart started pounding. I struggled to control it. I have historically not been a "sensitive" person, but I realized during this time that I wasn't "not sensitive." I was just numb and self-medicating my grief with perfectionism. Eventually my nervous system regulated again, but it took about a full year of my suddenly having to deal with depression and anxiety, which were not things I had ever felt overwhelmed by before.

I was obsessed with making meaning of my dad's life by trying to finish his work in mine. I decided I would stop trying to be busy and start trying to be present with my own thoughts. It was awful. And I let it be awful. I was flailing my arms and legs just to keep floating. But I wasn't floating. I was drowning. I was in deep water.

For the ancient Israelites, water appeared in lots of the stories that impacted the gods of their neighbors.[2] The Babylonians and Canaanites had mythology about their gods in battles with the waters, and the children of Israel would have heard about them. Moses, whose name, by the way, literally means "he who is drawn [from water],"[3] would never enter the land he had spent the last forty years preparing the people for. It was surely only his passion that kept him serving in his calling. The same Moses who got to lead the people on dry ground as God parted the sea would finish his ministry by dying in the desert. These are two very different mental images we will see throughout our time together, the juxtaposition of desert and water, and yet the same faithful God.

Water was a culturally relevant symbol in ancient times that may not have the same cultural impact as we read it today.

When people in ancient times heard *water*, they thought of monsters and the dangers of the deep. When I hear *water*, I think of Lake Michigan and days at the beach. If José would have told an ancient Israelite that God was taking them to deep water, they might have immediately imagined obstacles. But that was not the metaphor my brain offered me.

Last week I sat down for worship and remembered my mentor's words: "God is taking you to deeper water." I laughed out loud.

I said to God, "I thought that meant richer blessings and greater favor!"

There I was, cackling at 5:00 a.m. in my living room, talking out loud to God about what a fool that girl four years ago had been. And then I heard a still, small whisper. Hearing God for me is almost always a whisper. It is like hearing my own thoughts, but I don't think it's from me, because it often interrupts my own line of thinking.

I taught you how to swim. The thought dropped into my head like an anchor.

I started to cry. I'm not a swimmer. I like to lie on the beach or ride on a boat. You'll never see me in Cabo on a family vacation heading down to the pool to do laps. One time I hit a strong current while swimming in the water with my friends in high school and I literally let myself sink. I fought it for a minute and then I just lost the will. My friend Cassandra grabbed me and pulled me up.

"What the heck are you doing?" she scolded me. "Can't you swim?"

I knew a swimmer once who told me that if you chew gum while swimming, you are working every single muscle in your body. I have no idea if this is true, but in my brain, it tracks. Swimming is exhausting. Water is cold. Waves are scary. And yet here I am, and here you are, swimming. And when water is a metaphor for obstacles, then swimming takes on a whole new meaning.

Maybe nothing has gone as planned for you either. Maybe you are screaming to God that you'll drown. Maybe the current has taken you thirty-five miles off the coast, and you don't know if you'll have enough strength in your arms to keep lifting them. Maybe you gave up and decided it would be easier, and quieter, just to sink. Dear one, we *are* swimming. The Lord has taken us to deep water. And while this is outside of our comfort zone, maybe we should stop fighting against the current. Maybe we should just let it be awful, because it is. No numbing. Just presence.

Psalm 42:7–8 reads, "Deep calls to deep in the roar of your waterfalls; all your waves and breakers have swept over me. By day the LORD directs his love, at night his song is with me—a prayer to the God of my life."

I texted José and said,

Do you remember saying God was taking me to deeper water? I thought that meant richer blessings. As it turns out, it meant that God was going to teach me how to swim. And friend, I am swimming. I now know that even if everything goes wrong, even if I fail, even in deep grief, I am a woman who will get up at 5:00 a.m. and get back on my knees. I know how to walk when my legs are numb. I know how to pray when I am not sure anyone is listening. I know how to swim.

I texted him just over one hundred words and he texted me back with seven.

"You are equipped to swim," he said. "Be unafraid."

And that was it. No pleasantries or inspirational speeches. No "How you doing?" Or "Should we check back in?" Just an invitation to do what I was equipped to do. Get my butt back in the water. Keep swimming. I wrote it on the board that hangs in my office: "Be unafraid."

Being unafraid isn't about avoiding our fear but rather having courage despite it. One thing about life is you'll have to learn what to do in the water with a strong current. You can't get through this earthly journey without being surrounded by disorder and drenched in fear. Ever since Genesis, humanity has been met by chaos.

Welcome to deep water. You are equipped to swim. Be unafraid.

Deep calls to deep in the roar of your waterfalls; all your waves and breakers have swept over me. By day the LORD directs his love, at night his song is with me—a prayer to the God of my life.

Psalm 42:7–8

DIVE DEEPER

1. What obstacles are you facing?
2. What does "deep water" bring to your imagination?
3. Do you feel equipped to swim?

CHAPTER 3

KEEP SWIMMING

TEARS RAN DOWN MY FACE, BUT IT WAS HARD to tell because I was still wet from the pool. I pulled my bathing suit off while huddling next to my tiny locker, hoping not to draw attention to myself. My hair was stiff from chlorine. I should have rinsed it more, but all I wanted to do was get out of there. I was only eleven.

I tried to work the knots out of my hair. The comb felt heavy. I finally put the mess of tangles into a bun on the top of my head. The locker room had so much moisture in the air, it was getting hard to breathe. Swallowing felt thick. I put socks on my damp feet and shuffled my way up the stairs. Do you know the feeling of pulling dry clothes over wet skin? It feels like friction, like resistance. I avoid that feeling at all costs.

I had just taken the last swim test before I could start the final classes that preceded lifeguard training. The older, cooler kids all did lifeguard training. With any luck I would be one of them. My mother had put me in swimming lessons for several years.

"It's an important survival skill," she said. "Everyone should know how to swim."

I am not sure if she knew back then how true that statement was. What do we do when the chaotic waters of life surround us, threatening to undo all that we have done? Everyone should know how to swim. I looked at my piece of paper one last time before shoving it in my backpack.

Failed, it said in red pen.

Why do we do that? Why do we put scores, and grades, and marks in red? The words themselves carry more than enough weight without that added emphasis. Do we really need a color proven to create a physiological response? I heard once that most mammals can't see the color red. This is a problem because the color itself is meant to communicate danger. You see a red snake, and you instinctively know its bite could be poisonous. Words like *disappointment*, *rejection*, and *failure* can draw a fatal blow too. They can have you seeing red.

I walked down the stairwell to the exit and opened the large glass door, bolting right past my fellow swimmers without even a hint of caution. That's what we do before we know what it feels like to fall. We run in whatever direction we please. We bolt without even thinking about our steps. We flow wherever our dreams and adrenaline can carry us. In adulthood, all that stops. Dreams don't carry you. You carry them . . . cautiously.

I had two kids by the time I was twenty-six. My husband and I got pregnant on our honeymoon, which is honestly a topic for a different book. He was working as a carpenter. I was in graduate school and teaching part-time. We were so poor that my sister would often drop diapers on our doorstep and then pretend it wasn't her. On more than one occasion I had no idea how we would pay our mortgage. We were living on prayers and coupons. I made rice and beans almost every night for dinner. I was drowning in diaper changes and textbooks, so you can imagine my surprise when my husband came home one day and told me he wanted to go back to school.

"I have always dreamed of serving youth. Either as a teacher or a pastor," he said to me one evening.

My husband is an excellent carpenter. He has made us more money using those skills than he probably ever could in a serving profession. I am not at all knocking serving professions. I was a professor for almost fifteen years. But these fields, in general, do not make you wealthy. If Seth had opened his own carpentry business, we could've avoided some late fees. *Let's get an investor and start flipping houses.* That was the type of dreaming that would have excited me.

But my husband, in addition to being very skilled with a jigsaw, is also a steadfast mentor. He had been an at-risk youth who would not have survived his childhood traumas if not for caring Christian adults who invested in him. He wanted to give to other kids what people had given to him. That, to this day, is his passion. Passion, though, doesn't keep even rice and beans on the table. We had two babies under two. How could he dream of going back to school while I was still in school myself? Was this a marriage or a dorm room?

We prayed about it, and the next thing I knew, my husband was walking the same hallways I was teaching in. As an adult student at a community college, he sat in desks next to seventeen-year-old kids who were dual enrolled at their high schools. He made a choice at twenty-six to go back and do what so many of these other kids had done at seventeen: pursue passion. I am using *passion* here in the correct sense of the word. Nothing about those years was easy. His dreams didn't carry him across that stage at graduation. He had carried them, class by class, semester by semester, one grueling step at a time. My husband is resilient. He learned how to swim. He showed me what it looked like to be unafraid.

I can still remember being eleven years old and walking out those glass doors that held my swimming lesson failure. The air whipped through my wet hair. Who took swimming lessons in November anyway?

That was the first November I remember failing a test the Lord would repeat over and over in my life, for many Novembers to come. It was a test of whether I was willing to get back in the pool.

Do you have tests that you find yourself repeating over and over again? Here are some I'd like to bypass, but God and I must be on different wavelengths. These are the same tests we will be circling over and over in different ways throughout the following chapters.

- What do I do with failure?
- What do I do with disappointment?

- What do I do when God doesn't respond in the way
  I thought he would?
- Can I trust God when I feel like he is not fair?
- When will I ever believe I am good enough?
- What am I actually passionate about?
- What dreams are still worth carrying?

These tests, for me, started at age eleven. When did yours start?

I parked my car before a speaking engagement last week. I wanted to do a prayer walk but I didn't know the area. Prayer walks, for me, are exactly how they sound. It is a practice I began many years ago (see the appendix if you want more information on how I incorporate prayer walks as a spiritual practice). I started doing them because I had so much anxiety that I couldn't sit still, so I started walking around my block and talking to God about what was on my heart. I now do them even without anxiety. I walk and tell God I am grateful. I walk and remind myself of memories of God's provision. I walk and I speak Bible verses out loud that I want to claim over my life or children or circumstances. Few days go by that I am not walking with God. Before I spoke at that engagement, I walked in circles around an empty medical center parking lot. I had called Seth and something he mentioned was what made me want to pull over in the first place. He had been praying for me, and he had asked God, *Lord, Heather loves to make moments for other people. Today would you make a moment for her?*

Something about that sentence made tears well in my eyes. I tilted my head up so I wouldn't ruin my mascara. I parked my car and walked three laps around the lot, praying for the Holy Spirit and asking God to "make a moment" for me. On my third lap around the lot, it hit me what the date was: November 1. I've had so many painful Novembers. I could list off for you, year by year, the way that month had haunted me throughout my life. Breakups, disappointments, heartaches, grief, shame, embarrassment, broken promises, delayed dreams. Do you have a month like that? Or maybe for you it's a location or a holiday—your own personal Groundhog Day that triggers your brain into repeating unwelcome patterns. Where the date creeps up and the calendar reveals what your body had already remembered.

"Lord, please redeem all my Novembers," I said with my arms outstretched to heaven.

He could start with November 1998 and that crumpled failure slip in my backpack.

When I left the pool that day, I got to the bottom of the stairs and saw my dad's car was parked right at the rail. That's the beauty of childhood for those of us who had decent ones. When you fall, there is always someone to catch you. It's probably what makes taking risks a little safer. You know if everything goes bad, your parents will be somewhere in the parking lot. Maybe that's why I pulled into that empty parking lot before my speaking engagement. I was hoping God would catch me.

I knew before I even opened the car door that day in '98 that the temperature inside would be warm. Every room my dad was in was warm.

"Did you pass?" he asked as I slumped into the passenger seat, turning the heat toward my face.

I could feel the hum of the engine in his blue, 1994 Lincoln Town Car. To this day, when I think of my dad, I think of that car. My sister and I called it "the boat." It was four years old at this point, but it had the most spacious leather seats, and I swear it took up both lanes. My tears hit my face again. I didn't try to hide them.

"I failed," I moaned, letting my head hit the dashboard. "And everyone is going to know I failed," I added, which of course made failing that much more excruciating.

"Oh, I'm sorry, Heather," my dad said while maneuvering the boat across the lanes.

"But you must keep swimming."

His car was moving so slow it felt like we weren't going anywhere. Being with my dad was like that. It was like time was always stopping for him. You could hold your breath and lose count.

"Pass or fail," he said, keeping his eyes on the road ahead of him, "all that matters is that you keep swimming."

I didn't keep swimming. I never signed up for lessons again after that day in November, and now I'm a grown woman who can't beat her kids in a race from one side of the pool to the other. How's that for resilience?

Today, one of my best friends, Vimbo, called me. "Heather," she said, "your direction is more important than your speed."

And the second she said it, I remembered driving slowly down back roads with my dad in his 1994 Lincoln Town Car. I remembered that failure in November. I remembered my husband deciding to go back to school at twenty-six. Vimbo was talking to me about adult stuff. About careers and finances and office spaces and ministries and passion. About hustle culture and quitting jobs. About trying again after failure. Her point was heavy and precise, and it nearly made me drop my phone in my lap. But while she spoke of big-kid dilemmas, my brain remembered my dad's solution for his child.

"Just keep swimming."

I don't know what leap you are about to take. I don't know what dreams you have decided to start carrying. I don't know what November you may be sitting in. But I know that there is fresh water on the other side of every failure. I know that passion is a front stroke against the current. I know that you can choose to just keep swimming.

And I also know that more important than our speed is our direction.

He makes me lie down in green pastures, he leads me beside quiet waters.

Psalm 23:2

DIVE DEEPER

1. When have you experienced failure?
2. When have you experienced disappointment?
3. Why is our direction more important than our speed?

CHAPTER 4

IN THE BELLY
OF THE FISH

WHEN YOU SIT IN A DARK ROOM LONG ENOUGH, your iris expands your pupil. It is your body's way of dilating your eye so it can be more sensitive to the light. Within as little as twenty to thirty minutes, you will undergo something scientists call dark adaptation. It's when your eyes adjust to their new surroundings. You can see where you once couldn't. You adapted to the darkness. Many of us have gone years navigating the balance between what we believed God would do and the reality of what has been done. You can't walk that uncertainty without adapting to its darkness.

I remember sitting with a student of mine who wanted to go into film. She was an immigrant who was trying to explain to her hardworking parents that the creative arts offered her a sense of purpose that truly was worth suffering for.

"I told them," she said, sitting cross-legged on my office couch, "that either I am thirty-five years old, living in LA and doing this from my mansion, or I am thirty-five years old, living in LA and doing this from a van. Either way, I am pursuing film."

She was passionate. Pursuing film brought a joy that she was willing to suffer for. It wasn't about accolades or titles. It was about what the process of telling visual stories did within her own soul. She had thrown caution to the wind.

The *Oxford English Dictionary* defines *passion* as a "barely controllable emotion."[1] Some of us can't control ourselves when it comes to our passions. We are compelled to chase an extreme. It doesn't matter if the water raises us toward the sky or sweeps us up beneath it. We are going to greet the wave.

For a moment, I had considered warning my student of the danger of wading out into the deep. I knew firsthand what happens when your feet can no longer touch the ground. Next thing you know, you're drowning.

The Roman poet Ovid tells the legend of Icarus, who was the son of an inventor named Daedalus. The story goes that Daedalus is hired by the king of Crete to build a labyrinth. Eventually, however, he falls into disfavor with the king and is condemned, with Icarus, to spend the rest of his life inside the maze. Being an incredible inventor, Daedalus comes up with a plan to escape. That's what creators do. They find ways to help us escape whatever maze we have been wandering in. They find ways to break us free of the same old patterns we've grown used to.

Daedalus constructs wings. He ties them together using feathers and wax. He is solving a problem with a practical solution. Together, the two will leave the maze. Daedalus sees this as a way of escape, but Icarus sees it as a way to freedom. There is a difference between escape and freedom. One has you running from, the other has you running to.

Daedalus gives Icarus some instructions for how to use his new wings. For us, too, wings, just like passion, must come with instructions. You can't just put them on and expect to know what to do. You must be cautioned. Wings fit on your skin just like dreams do. You can allow them just enough air to escape the maze you are running from, or you can stretch them out and soar. Icarus thought wings should do what they were made to do: let you fly to freedom. His father didn't see it that way.

"Don't fly too low, and don't fly too high," Daedalus warned, because he knew warnings would be necessary.

If he flew too low, the ocean would wet the wings and they might not recover. And if he flew too high, the heat of the sun would melt the wax, and the wings that carried them would disintegrate. Icarus was just a boy. He had the youthful naivety that so many of us once had. It's almost as if his story isn't only his—not once you sit quietly and read it to yourself. One minute you are where you are, and the next, you are sleeping in his bed. Your hands are dirty with wax and feathers. That's what stories often do.

Icarus wanted to see what life was like above the ground. He had lived so long inside that maze. He took off, like young people often do. Gliding above the water, then soaring above the trees. The higher he went, the freer he felt. He was more concerned with how to fly than with what happens when you fall. He lost himself in those wings. The power of flight took over.

Daedalus was also flying, but slowly, with a great deal of caution, and only because he had to in order to escape.

And yet, as he went, he lost sight of Icarus. He peered toward the clouds and saw no sign of the young boy he had warned so intensely. Adults love to warn us when we are young of the danger of getting ahead of ourselves. *Accidents happen when you lose control. Stick to what's safe. Keep your wings far below the sun. Who will catch you if you fall?*

But Icarus got lost in the power of his own wind. The higher he got, the more he could see. The world looks different when you see it from the vantage point of the sky. Everything you thought was so important suddenly becomes incredibly small. Safety and security are a high price to pay for what Icarus was able to experience. He found freedom from the labyrinth. His passion took him where only passion can take you: all the way to the sun. And that's the danger of flying. You don't realize you can fall. Suddenly the wax that had been holding his wings together went dripping down his side. He had gotten too close to the sun. And just like that, his feathers fell, fluttering downward.

Falling feels like flying, he thought. But then he vanished into the sea.

Daedalus started to panic. Surely his son hadn't chased the extremes.

"Icarus!" he yelled.

Daedalus was very careful to keep his emotions measured. He knew not to lose himself in the wind. Looking down, he saw the crashing waves beneath him. The ocean is a dangerous place for people whose anatomy includes legs and feet. Adults know the risks of swimming. We know that we may drown. And so, the story goes, there, in the uncertainty of the sea, Daedalus saw a small cluster of feathers floating on the water. It was all that was left of Icarus. Except, of course, for the story that would be saved by the poet. A tale of caution. A caveat of chasing after extremes.

It's a warning to the young and a familiar song to the old. That passion is best controlled. That wings can't carry you as safely as legs can. Dreams are for the sky. Live your life between the extremes. Don't let your hopes take you beyond where your feet can touch. Your imagination is just hallucinations. It's crazy to leave the ground.

We have been telling the story of Icarus ever since. It reminds us of the dangers of passion and cautions us about pursuing our dreams. And everywhere the story got told, the message would remain the same. That children should stay on the ground. It would be safer in the maze. This was the lesson to the young about what happens when you fly so high you touch the sun or so low you skim the water. Because water will do what water always does—swallow everything it meets. We see similar patterns in Genesis.

Chaotic waters in the Bible often reveal a space incompatible with life. It is the opposite of creation. Just ask Noah. And this thread continues outside of Genesis. We see it in Exodus with the army of Pharaoh meeting the Hebrew God of Moses and the Israelites in an epic biblical moment at the Red Sea. Moses raises his staff, and the Israelites walk on dry land. A rod or staff in the Bible was used by shepherds to guide their flock. It is, again, very important biblical imagery: God shepherding Israel out of bondage through his chosen vessel, Moses, by having them travel through the chaotic waters into the promised land. Creation and new creation. God brings order out of chaos.

We see it in Psalms. For example, Psalm 69:1–2 reads, "Save me, God, for the water has risen to my neck. I have sunk in deep mud, and there is no footing; I have come into deep water, and a flood sweeps over me" (csb). Here, water is symbolic of helplessness and danger. If only Icarus would have known.

David uses the same comparison in Psalm 18:16: "He reached down from on high and took hold of me; he pulled me out of deep water" (csb). Water here is a metaphor, meaning a tool of evil—and it is only God, the Creator in Genesis 1, who can provide us with salvation, though the waters of this world may rage.

We see it in the book of Jonah, where, after the prophet went in the opposite direction of the command of God, the waters found him. A violent storm came over the sea and left Jonah's pagan shipmates crying out to their gods. Jonah, while telling the crew who he was and about the God he worshipped, referred back to Genesis 1 and our story of creation.

Jonah 1:9 reads, "I'm a Hebrew. I worship the LORD, the God of the heavens, who made the sea and the dry land" (csb).

This may seem an odd comment for us in a twenty-first-century context, but keep in mind that many people worshipped the sun, the moon, or the stars during biblical times. Jonah was sharing with the pagan crew that his God was the one true God, the Creator of all things. Israelites, like Jonah, lived under a polytheistic cultural system. It is one of the reasons they pledged their allegiance to the one true God in a prayer called the Shema, every morning and every evening.[2]

The prayer is found in Deuteronomy 6:4–5 and it reads in the CSB, "Listen, Israel: The LORD our God, the LORD is one. Love the LORD your God with all your heart, with all your soul, and with all your strength." It should give you further context as to why Jesus responded the way he did when asked in Mark 12:29–31 which is the greatest commandment. He referenced the daily prayer of every Israelite, the Shema, but added that we are to love our neighbors as ourselves.

Jonah eventually instructed the crew to throw him overboard, and though they were reluctant, he told them that if they did, the water would calm. The prophet Jonah, much like Adam in Genesis, Israel in general, and probably you and me, chose not to keep God's command. He was unfaithful and probably should have drowned in the chaotic waters of the sea. That's what water often does in these stories. It brings destruction on the wicked. But the Lord, who brings order where there is chaos, sent a great fish to deliver Jonah from the depths.

It is there, from the belly of the fish, that Jonah experienced dark adaptation. His eyes adjusted to the new light he had been given, and he prayed a prayer that referred back to many of the psalms, just like the one we mentioned earlier, Psalm 69.

Jonah 2:5 reads, "The water engulfed me up to the neck; the watery depths overcame me" (csb).

It is reminiscent of Psalm 69:1–2: "Save me, God, for the water has risen to my neck. I have sunk in deep mud, and there is no footing; I have come into deep water, and a flood sweeps over me" (csb). The prophet was repeating the words of the great King David of Israel.

Then, from the depths of the sea, Jonah promised to carry out his original mission to preach to the people of Nineveh. Jonah was reborn. Creation and new creation. God brings order out of chaos. Jonah has been redeemed. The water that should have destroyed him had actually washed him clean. It is a perfect illustration of the themes of water in the Bible. Remember, God is never threatened by the waters that threaten us. Within God is a river of life.

I have been in the belly of the fish, so to speak. I have felt the water rising to my neck. And sometimes in the belly of the fish, unlike Jonah, I don't even have a prayer. I sit with God and don't say anything at all. I've gone on morning prayer walks where I don't even pray. There are a thousand things I could say, but it feels like I have already said them. So, I don't say anything. I just walk or sit in complete silence. It is my way of showing God I am still here; I am just in the belly of the fish. I don't have strength to praise him through the storm or enough faith to prophesy over the mountain. But I have just enough left in me to show up. To be present. To circle the block one more time. To sit in silence and let what is awful be awful because it is.

Sometimes faith is in our feelings, and other times faith is in our feet. It is in our ability to not be afraid of all the quiet. To show up when you have nothing left to bring besides yourself. No gifts. No songs. No rehearsed scriptures. Just you. And somewhere in all that silence, being certain that it is enough. I found out while in the belly of the fish that prayer isn't always about talking. Sometimes it's about being. You are still here. And that is enough.

"I'm drowning," I wrote in my prayer journal.

What I didn't know then is what I want to share with you now. That sometimes, the very thing you thought would destroy you can wash over you and make you clean. The covenant of God still stands over your life. No matter what happens in these deep waters, God will keep the promise with himself. We can pledge our allegiance to the one true God who made the sun, the moon, the stars, and the dry land. Morning and evening, no matter what comes, we, too, can repeat the Shema. "Listen, Israel: The LORD our God, the LORD is one. Love the LORD your God with all your heart, with all your soul, and with all your strength."

The Christian life is about creation and new creation. It's about risk and redemption. It's about joy and suffering—dreams that die so that passion can live. It's about waves that come up to our necks and about what it feels like to lose your footing in the mud.

To live with passion is to experience extremes, or else it was never passion or living at all. All of us will eventually fly too close to the sun. All of us will meet the belly of the whale.

Jonah prayed to the LORD his God from the belly of the fish: "I called to the LORD in my distress, and he answered me. I cried out for help from deep inside Sheol; you heard my voice."

Jonah 2:1–2 CSB

DIVE DEEPER

1. What does it mean to you to know that God is Creator?
2. Where in your life are you taking on "water"?
3. Have you ever been in the "belly of the fish"?

CHAPTER 5

THE PARK FACING THE WATER

WHEN I WAS TWENTY-FIVE, I HIT ANOTHER November. The old, familiar test swept over me like a wave. *What do I do with failure? What do I do with disappointment?* Hello, Groundhog Day.

This time I lost my job. I honestly didn't realize that jobs were something good workers could lose. Adulthood loves to reveal to us how much there is to learn. I was teaching at a college, and due to some staff rearranging I was going to have to share an office with a very important administrator's wife. I was told that she didn't want to share an office with me. I couldn't fault her for that. This wasn't Google. Give me some cinder block and privacy. Look, girl, I get it.

Unfortunately for me, though, my college decided that one of the ways to alleviate the need for a shared office was to cut my position. I had a small lecturer salary that I would now lose as I transitioned to an adjunct or part-time worker. I also wouldn't be given an office. I had been promised that in one more year, a budget had already been approved that would move me to full-time instructor. I was counting on that promotion. I had already made an offer on a house because of it.

With an official letter from my department chair that I could give to my bank, Seth and I put an offer on what was going to be our first home. I had a one-year-old and was pregnant with my second child, a little boy we would eventually name Hudson. However, in one email from the chair of my department, I lost everything. I did not know until talking with my chair in person that the reason I was losing my job was because someone's wife didn't want to share an office with me. I sincerely couldn't believe what was happening or that something like that was even possible. I lost what was supposed to be my coming full-time position, I lost my part-time lecturer salary, and I lost my home. They said I could keep doing the same job for next to no pay and no office. Thank you so much for the opportunity, but I declined. I am a millennial. We believe in fair wages.

I spent nearly every day that fall sitting on a bench at a park that faced the lake, watching the turtles. They say that turtles have an internal compass that leads them in the direction of water. That's the thing about turtles. They know that direction is more important than speed. I think I have something like that in me. Something instinctual that drives me to the water's edge. I'd take my daughter and my pregnant belly and stare at the lake while rocking back and forth on one of those porch swings that sat up on a hill. I probably looked like a madwoman. Someone watching would have worried I was a ghost.

The lady in black, wailing in the wind, rocking on that swing, facing the water, clutching my daughter. I had worked so hard and was so close to my dreams, and then, in a single day, I lost everything. I had flown too close to the sun.

I was experiencing passion. We think that if we do everything right, life won't still happen to us. We think that we can somehow avoid disruption if we are just faithful and quiet and keep our heads down and do the work. This has not been my experience. Life simply refuses to be fair. I have been minding my own business and still been dragged out by the current. Sometimes bad things happen to good people, and at least in my experience it has been futile to try to figure out the theology of a world in chaos.

The chaotic water is bigger than all of us, and we will never understand on this side of glory why there are seasons where the good suffer and the wicked triumph. A theology that gives perfect answers on suffering probably hasn't experienced it. Jesus seems to believe that compassion doesn't belong to the good; it simply belongs. He taught that grace and mercy aren't earned; they are freely given. It is interesting, though, that the God who says that the sun shines on both the evil and the good would live in that tension his entire life and ministry (Matthew 5:45). It would take the passion of Christ to keep pursuing the very same world that would place him on a cross. Jesus' messaging regarding suffering and chaos is never empty. He lived every word he preached. He faced both the wind and the waves.

It changes how I see Matthew 14, where Jesus walks on water in the midst of a storm. I hope this story has an even heavier significance for you now that you understand the imagery of water in the Bible. It is God who subdues the chaos. It is God who brings order both then and now. Jesus is not just doing this miracle because it looks cool. He is revealing himself to the disciples. The same disciples who in Mark 4:38 said, "Teacher, don't you care if we drown?"

They asked this question to the God of Genesis who created the sea and the dry land. Jesus revealed to them that he has power over the storm. Jesus is living water. He both walked on water and hung on a cross. He revealed himself as both God of creation and God of the covenant.

John 19:34 in the CSB reads, "But one of the soldiers pierced his side with a spear, and at once blood and water came out." This water is symbolic of the keeping of the covenant. Through the death of Jesus all of humanity has the invitation to experience new life. A renewing water, like in Genesis 2:10: "A river went out from Eden to water the garden" (CSB). Jesus restores the Edenic promise. His life brings living water to all of the earth.

Did you know that the English word *testament*, as in Old and New Testament, is derived from a Greek word that actually means "covenant"?[1] A covenant is essentially an agreement. In ancient times, this term was used to describe an agreement between a king and his people. A king would promise to protect and provide, and the people would promise their loyalty. The terms of that promise were expressed in the covenant.

The Bible, then, comprises more than the Old and New Testaments; it also comprises the old and new covenant. As someone who studied communication for over a decade, I think that language is incredibly important. A dramatic shift happens in the agreement between King (God) and people (Israel). Probably the most shocking is that while the terms of the agreement aren't necessarily kept on the part of the people of Israel, they are kept on the part of the King.

Jesus would be born a man and allow himself to be crucified wearing a crown of thorns. Jesus is standing in the place of both King and people. He is both the covenant Creator and covenant Redeemer. God became man and kept the covenant with himself. I need you to remember this the next time you think you are drowning. Jesus walked on water.

Don't you care if I drown? I cried to God on a porch swing overlooking the lake. *Why couldn't you protect me?*

My husband and I were so poor at this time that he literally worked for food. He painted my friends' living room and bedroom in exchange for groceries. It truly felt like God had left me unprotected. I was a good teacher. I was committed to my students. I was a keep-your-head-down-and-do-the-work colleague. And yet I lost my livelihood because someone who was more important than me had a wife who didn't want to share an office.

I think in some ways this became my origin story. The tiny villain inside me that would whisper cruel words at every shortcoming for the rest of my life. *You will never be good enough. You are unimportant. Look at how hard your husband has to work now because of you. You are a failure.* I had become someone who was easily discarded. My life, to everyone else, felt like an afterthought. I was an unemployed mother of two with two graduate degrees and no office.

Seth and I had walked that home we thought was ours so many times. I can still see the dining room in it where I had envisioned our kids experiencing Christmas in the first home that would truly be ours. Every now and then I still drive by that house. It was walking distance to the water. My internal compass must have chosen it. I wonder what our lives would have been like if we hadn't lost that home. It is not an exaggeration to say that our entire lives today would look different if I had not lost that job. It put into motion a chain of reactionary events that changed what I do and who I am today. It was one of what would become many heartbreaks. I was back in a parking lot, but it felt like there was no warm car to jump into. Just the chill of November.

Those days marked the beginning for me of coming to the lake. I've been doing it ever since. Something about the water made the pain dampen. There is something about watching waves break that honors the brokenness in your own body. I had put my identity in my job title. I didn't know who I was without it. It's interesting, isn't it? How at first we are children who like to do things, and then we become adults who are defined by what we do? I wasn't sure if I was still me if I wasn't a professor. That was the person I had spent so much of my energy trying to become. Someone who looked important.

That year my internal compass led me to the water. And it has taken me more than a decade to understand what kept propelling me to that lake. All I wanted, what I most deeply needed, was a feeling that only water offered: the ability to become weightless.

We have talked about the "chaos" of water, but can I take a moment to explore with you some of the calm of water? Something happens when we step into it. It is unnerving to be a part of something that is so much bigger than you are. I suppose that is what chaos reminds us of. That we are not in control of much. That passion is heavy. That all of us are a drop in the ocean of this world.

But I also find it interesting that the same water that can consume you can remove all your weight. Everything is lighter in the sea. You discover you can carry more. Perhaps that is true of all chaos. The same water that can break you can form you. There has never been a really light and easy season of my life when I grew exponentially. Only difficulty has gifted me that. When I think back over my experiences, it is not the winning that has formed my character as much as the seasons where I had to figure out how to lose and yet keep swimming. Passion, in its truest sense of the word, will reveal to you what was inside you all along. That's all that pressure does—reveal what was already inside.

I would like you to speak a prayer out loud as you find yourself treading water from Psalm 69:13. It reads, "But as for me, LORD, my prayer to You is for a time of favor. In Your abundant, faithful love, God, answer me with Your sure salvation" (CSB). Throughout our journey together, that is what I am praying over you: A time of favor. A season of weightlessness. But in the meantime, I hope it helps you to know that you are not alone.

That even your biblical heroes knew what it felt like to be sure they would drown.

While I sat on the bench at the park facing the water, I remember saying out loud to God, "I don't know who you are anymore." And as sure as my tears were falling, this thought dropped into my head that interrupted my line of thinking and would change how I faced difficulty in life ever since.

What do you know?

That was it.

When we are in a moment that tests what we think we know to be true about who God is or how God works, we must remind our brains of what we *do* know. When there are many things you don't know, you have to actively say out loud what you *do* know. And we know that the God in Joseph's pit is the same God in Joseph's palace. And that the God in Moses' failure is the same God who strengthened his faith. The God of Hannah's wailing is the same God of Hannah's worship. And the God who David called out to when he felt he was drowning is the same God who defended him before Goliath.

I have Psalm 69:14–18 highlighted in my Bible. I am telling you, once you see the theme of water in Scripture, you notice it everywhere.

Rescue me from the miry mud; don't let me sink. Let me be rescued from those who hate me and from the deep waters. Don't let the floodwaters sweep over me or the deep swallow me up; don't let the Pit close its mouth over me. Answer me, LORD, for Your faithful love is good. In keeping with Your abundant compassion, turn to me. Don't hide Your face from Your servant, for I am in distress. Answer me quickly! Draw near to me and redeem me; ransom me because of my enemies. (CSB)

It was when I lost my job and my house fell through that I started going to the park to sit with God and watch the water. Looking back, that practice would change the entire trajectory of the rest of my life. Sometimes when the pressure of the waves surrounds us, it only reveals what has been inside us all along. Because that's what both water and passion do to us. They break and they form. They strip and they reveal. They bring both chaos and calm. My prayer for you is for a time of favor. May the Lord, in his abundant, faithful love, answer you with his sure salvation.

When you pass through the waters,
　　I will be with you;
　　and when you pass through the rivers,
　　they will not sweep over you.

Isaiah 43:2

DIVE DEEPER

1. What is a moment in your life that created a series of reactionary events?
2. How do you speak back to negative internal voices?
3. Where do you go to feel "weightless"?

CHAPTER 6

GOD COUNTS

THERE IS A FINE LINE BETWEEN FAITH AND delusion. I can't always tell which side of it I'm on. I come by it honestly. I am my father's daughter. I saw my dad every morning before I saw the sun. He'd tiptoe past my room to the basement. My sister and I called it "the dungeon." It was dark down there, and quiet. It had old carpet that was sometimes damp if it had rained a lot the night before. There were no windows except for those little basement windows you could debatably fit your body through if there was a fire. Tiny, fogged shafts of light broke through what was otherwise darkness. It was hardly the place one would go to meet with God. And yet that dungeon was exactly where Dad went every morning to meet with God.

From the time I was in third grade until I moved into my first apartment at twenty-one, I watched my dad's feet quietly trail down the hallway and then disappear into the basement. He'd read his Bible for hours down there, and when he prayed, he would place his face on that old carpet. My dad didn't just pray, he groaned. It could be hours before he reappeared upstairs. I never saw somebody try to grab hold of the throne of God like that. Faith can do that to us. It can cause us to pray like people who have lost themselves. I couldn't understand back then what would possess someone to pray like that. You'd have thought he'd killed somebody. But now I know that hope had been slowly killing him. He was grasping around at wax and feathers, trying to pray for wings. I now know because I've lived it. The point where passion meets pain.

I bought my second home in 2015. It had a three-season porch that was all windows. I would take my Bible out there and face the woods. I'd get on my knees on that porch before the daylight. I underlined and highlighted while listening to the birds. I'd take a blanket and a heater in winter. Nothing stopped me from edging my way out onto that porch. It was my favorite room in the entire house. I met with God there. And now I can't help but wonder if that was the first time I tried to create space between my faith and my dad's.

Have you ever thought you heard God tell you something about your future? Maybe it's a word or a dream or a vision that gets planted in your spirit like a seed. It's a promise that God speaks over you, and in the beginning you believe wholeheartedly. You protect that little seed at all costs. You cup your hands around it like you'd cradle a baby bird. You can feel its heat as you hold it.

"Say less, God!" we respond. "Your servant is listening." "Here I am, Lord. Send me!"

At first, we know exactly what we heard. Nothing can shake us out of the calling we feel. We are Daniel unafraid in the face of lions or we're Joshua in Jericho. We know what we felt the Lord placed on our hearts, and we will not back down. That seed grows throughout the years. It sits like a marker that becomes a defining moment for your entire life. Its branches give you a place to rest. Its leaves shade you. But then as time passes and you don't see very much fruit, you start to question if you heard correctly.

Did I make that up? we wonder. *Maybe I was wrong,* we rationalize. Year after year we check our tree, looking for a visible sign or blessing. Season by season we parse through leaves. We place our hands at the roots hoping to feel that heat. Eventually we have a choice to make. *Do I let this go? Do I cut the very branch I've been sitting on? Should hope hurt like this?*

That's when the prayers start to change. That's when the groans come. After Joseph interpreted the baker and cupbearer's dreams, he sat in prison for another two years before the cupbearer remembered to bring his name to Pharaoh (Genesis 40–41). For years he checked his tree. Season after season it bore no fruit. *Maybe my dream was wrong?* I'm sure Joseph wondered. The Bible doesn't give us the exact number of years in total that Joseph sat in prison before meeting the cupbearer and baker, but we can rest assured that Joseph kept count. It's often the only thing we can control. The ability to keep count.

Do you remember when you started counting? When exactly did your life become marked by years? Time used to be invisible for me. Do you remember that? When the passing of time meant nothing to you? When days didn't come with a map? When there was no thought of *how long* it has been? When you didn't know exactly how many months had passed between your hope and disappointment? Time was all around us, surely, but we didn't pay attention. We didn't have to. Not until our lives were marked by it.

Anniversaries are a strange thing. Happy ones give us exciting years to keep track of, but what about the unhappy ones? What happens when we count those? What about the years in Joseph's prison? Or the months spent treading water? What about the trips around the sun we've taken while waiting on God to move? What happens when we start counting how long between the desert and the promised land? Those anniversaries mark us too. They cause us to count. And once you start counting, it is very hard to stop.

Days are never just days anymore, and years are never just years. Because you know how many. You know how many days, months, years have passed since the first time or the last time you experienced whatever your anniversary is meant to track. I have a few different anniversaries. Days I feel like my life changed for the good or for the bad, for one reason or another. Days that made my prayer life change. Days that forced me onto the porch before the sun. Days that made me groan.

I mark them, in some ways, even before I understand just how much they will mark me. But we aren't the same people we were before the water came flooding in. Joseph surely didn't exit the prison the same man he was when he went in. "How long, Lord?" becomes something observable. We count now. Time is no longer invisible. Invisibility is a luxury. In some ways that marking even impacts how we experience the future. You know how long before and how long since. You become obsessed with it.

Lord, I thought I'd have my husband by now, we murmur. *I swore you told me to write this book,* we groan. *Didn't you call me to this ministry?* we cry. *I asked you for direction before I started this business!* we yell. *Did I get here by faith? Or by delusion?* And then we check the calendar to see how long we have prayed this hard for this little. How long the maze has kept us stuck.

I wonder how long God has been counting. Since Genesis, surely. Order and time were the first act of creation. Genesis 1 says that God created the light and then separated it from the darkness. That was day one. The beginning of time. I find solace in the idea that God is a God of order. The true keeper of the count. All that is, and all that was, passes through the hands of God. A God who is unfazed by time. A God who brings order to chaos.

Second Peter 3:8–9 reads, "Dear friends, don't overlook this one fact: With the Lord one day is like a thousand years, and a thousand years like one day. The Lord does not delay his promise, as some understand delay, but is patient with you, not wanting any to perish but all to come to repentance" (CSB).

Other than you, God is the only person who knows exactly how long it has been. He is the only person patient enough to withstand the ticking hands of every clock. God, the Creator of light and darkness, the establisher of order and time, refuses to be rushed. Artistry often can't be. He knows how long you have hoped. He knows how many days you've spent on your knees in the dungeon. He has heard every single groan. The patience of an eternal God feels like a mystery to mortal beings. But there is something beautiful in endurance. Something that feels bigger than anything we can see.

Psalm 77:16–20 reads,

The water saw you, God. The water saw you; it trembled. Even the depths shook. The clouds poured down water. The storm clouds thundered; your arrows flashed back and forth. The sound of your thunder was in the whirlwind; lightning lit up the world. The earth shook and quaked. Your way went through the sea and your path through the vast water, but your footprints were unseen. You led your people like a flock by the hand of Moses and Aaron. (csb)

It's an incredible image in those verses. A God whose footsteps are invisible but whose hands are seen through his people. It's a reminder that God has chosen to be invisible because he is best seen through his people. We are his image bearers. Moses, Aaron, and Miriam would be called to lead the people through the chaotic waters long after they left Egypt. And part of walking fully in the image of God is to colabor in the work of God. Please note I have included Miriam not to make a feminist point but to be true to the Scriptures.

Micah 6:4 reads, "Indeed, I brought you up from the land of Egypt and redeemed you from that place of slavery. I sent Moses, Aaron, and Miriam ahead of you" (csb). Moses, Aaron, and Miriam passed through the waters and entered the wilderness. It's another theme of Scripture. Water and desert. We see echoes of Genesis in our interconnected scriptures, of the God who made the sea and the dry ground. I am sure once out of the chaos of Egypt, they thought the hard work was over, but it had only just begun.

The definition of *work* in the dictionary is "exertion or effort directed to produce or accomplish something."[1] My non-profit, It Is Day Ministries, was inspired by John 9:4, which reads, "We must work the works of him who sent me while it is day" (ESV). Living in your calling, continuing in your passion, colaboring with Christ, will be work. And work by definition will require the exertion of your effort. Work will always cost us something. But we don't strive as the world strives, because we know where to find our rest.

God created the moon and stars and the earth that circles around the sun. May we never forget, as we press our faces to the floor before the daylight, that the God of creation is the God of the covenant. There are no chaotic waters that we won't ultimately be delivered from, either in this life or the next. The Creator has heard every cry.

Six years ago, to the very day I am writing right now, over the course of forty days, I fasted three times, sat for hours with my Bible, and did countless prayer walks praying a prayer that, at the time, God never answered. I know that this happened only because Facebook memories reminded me. My caption on that day read, "My prayer partner and I will be concluding our forty days of prayer this weekend. We haven't seen God answer any of the things we prayed over, and yet, I no longer need to see God to know he is moving."

My friend Vimbo was single and praying to meet her husband. I was praying I could be a published author, which, after all the rejection letters I'd received, was a passion I was nearly ready to release. When we finished those forty days, we truly believed that nothing had happened. But as I write this to you six years later, Vimbo just texted me because her husband had single-handedly planned her birthday party, gotten a cake, and gathered friends together to celebrate his wife. As I read that text, I realized that God had remembered me too.

Vimbo's text message coming in, on the same day that my Facebook memory popped up, at the same time that I was writing this, feels like more than a coincidence—a Christ-incidence maybe. A not-so-subtle reminder that God was keeping count. That six years ago I was certain I had prayed over and over faithfully and nothing had happened. Vimbo got off her knees still single. I said "amen" with no glimmer of hope that my writing would ever be read by anyone besides my family. And yet, here we both are, six years later, living in the answer to prayers we prayed six years before. Artistry takes time. The Creator of order and time would know.

I don't know what circumstance you are sitting in the middle of that you are certain isn't changing. I don't know what prayer you've repeated that it feels like no one is hearing. But I do know that I had forgotten what I prayed six years ago, and today God revealed to me that he had been keeping count.

All that is broken will be redeemed. All groans will be washed with grace. All promises will be kept in the fullness of his time. For forty years Moses, who was drawn out of the water, would work for the Lord with passion in the wilderness. And in the new covenant, for forty days Jesus would also enter the wilderness. He is the living water in the desert, bringing new life to all who thirst. Because God keeps count. He created time before he created humanity. He set in motion the order of days and years, and there is something about remembering this that gives me peace to endure the season.

God knows how long it's been. God knows exactly how long you've waited. What God is building in our lives, he is patient to complete. This work will require the exertion of your effort. Can you endure for one more day?

Because I assure you, God counts.

"Indeed, the very hairs of your head are all numbered. Don't be afraid."

Luke 12:7

DIVE DEEPER

1. What painful anniversaries do you keep track of?
2. What is the difference between faith and delusion?
3. What does it mean when Heather says, "God counts"?

CHAPTER 7

THE SHORE

"I WANTED TO GIVE YOU THIS," A STUDENT SAID. She handed me a thank-you card with a note she had written about our semester together. We'd chatted in my office many times. She was navigating a decision to transfer out of our smaller Christian university into a bigger public university campus in a larger city. We talked about that some days. Other days we talked about her roommate, who had been her best friend in high school, but somehow they found themselves changing in college.

"People change," I told her. "We grow and sometimes we outgrow places and phases and people. It happens to everyone."

Her on-again, off-again boyfriend was doing a year abroad. The space had given her time to think through her own life, and she realized she wanted off our small campus into something bigger and less controlled.

"What if I go there and I fail?" she asked. "It's a really rigorous program. What if I can't keep up?"

She was scared that failure would ruin her life. I told her that failure was a part of it.

She hadn't felt nervous coming to the Christian university near the town she'd grown up in. She'd come because it was where her friends from high school were going. The nervous energy she was now experiencing about venturing out on her own was bringing up all different types of feelings, and none of them were feelings of safety. I told her she could trust herself to do what was best for her. And that I trusted her to do what was best for her. We prayed, and she left. And now here she was at the end of the semester, handing me a card. She was thanking me for giving her permission to feel fear and yet be unafraid. She left our school at the end of the semester and moved away to a big city.

It always starts with childhood, they say. Show me an adult listless and numb, and I'll show you a child who learned which end of the pool was safer. No one is born numb. We grow into it. It's like an old coat we try on. It's baggy, and doesn't fit, and has a smell that you know isn't yours. It's something borrowed. But you reach for it anyway, even though the texture is not familiar. You slip it on. At first because it's cold out here, and being cold is undesirable. There is nothing comfortable in a chill that moves its way up your spine uninvited. So you pull the coat around you and pretend that it fits. You are making the best of it. But then you just keep wearing it. You worry about what would happen if you took it off. You worry what would happen if you started to feel anything—even warm.

We aren't born afraid to feel the world around us. Our brains were born to process feelings. "Numb" is not a part of our emotions. It's a lack of them. It's an option we choose when we feel too much of everything else and lose the ability to put language to how or why. It all just gets tangled. We think it would be easier to just feel nothing. We become afraid of our own feelings. Our brains get overwhelmed and, in an attempt to protect us, shut everything down. But you weren't born like this. None of us was. You are born with two basic fears: the fear of falling and the fear of loud noises. Every other fear, we have taught ourselves by experience.[1]

Fear is a learned behavior. It's adaptive. It's how you learn how to navigate potential threats from people and your environment. It's an emotion we attach to past experiences, and we let it warn us should anything we see right now resemble what we saw back then. We talk about fear like it is something we need to overcome, but the reality is that fear should be treasured. In moderation, like all things, it's a gift to your personhood. It's how you remember which path not to take. It's how you learn which people aren't safe. Fear is not a dirty word, and you shouldn't feel bad for embracing it. It's how you have survived. It's why we like the shallows. But we can become unafraid.

I grew up on Lake Michigan. There is so much nostalgia to my adolescence. I walked piers before I had a driver's license. I had sand in my sheets for years. I loved to walk the stretch of shore or hike the dunes. It is cold up north for about nine months out of the year. For the three months you can go outside comfortably, you get as close as you can to the water. I have driven to the pier before work just to watch the waves. When I moved back to my hometown from Denver, property near the water was the only property I was interested in purchasing. For Michiganders, the lake is a sanctuary.

I didn't have a cell phone until my sophomore year of high school. So when I went to the lake as a kid, it was honestly like going to another planet. I kept a quarter in my bra for a pay phone. If no one answered, you died there. The lake was a place where no one could find you and yet everyone could find you. My sister's boyfriend would drop me off at the beach at 10:00 a.m. and pick me up after work close to 6:00 p.m. My parents abandoned me to the dunes. I was raised by waves. I ate hot dogs from carts and licked ice cream off my fingers. I can still see the faces of dozens and dozens of my classmates, their eyes dancing off the water. My life was one giant swim party. Our summers were spent swinging off ropes into fast-paced currents. It was dangerous, but we were immortal. Children always think they are.

In middle school, if I couldn't get out to Lake Michigan, I would settle for Lake Chapin. It's a small lake in the small Michigan town that raised me. We would swim out on Lake Chapin with fifteen of my closest friends. The laughter carried us further than the current. We didn't need a boat. Just our limbs and our lungs. There were large abutments in the middle of the lake. I would swim several hundred meters and then climb them. The ladder that you had to use was so old that every time you stepped onto it, you braced yourself for the ropes to snap. None of this was a deterrent. Which is odd, but only from my vantage point now.

I can see everything so much differently now. I am not sure if it is clearer or just a different view. Few things in life are truly one-dimensional. You are always just trading views. The water was freezing but the sun was warm. Both feelings could coexist back then. They didn't cancel each other out. I didn't have to choose, and I wasn't afraid to shiver. I am not sure when that happened exactly—when I started to choose feeling numb over feeling cold. As a child, being cold just felt like home.

Without a care in the world, I'd jump. I can still feel the wind pressing itself into my skin. My friends would cheer me on. My body cut through the water like a knife, yet nothing about the lake felt sharp back then. I was good at holding my breath. I don't think I ever touched the bottom. Chapin seemed so deep, like no matter how high you were, there was always more space to plunge. Swimming often feels like that. Like you could never reach the end. The water is limitless. An endless depth of potential.

It's funny, because back then, potential felt positive. And as I write the word out now, stringing along its letters, it brings back all my fears. I am so tired of endless potential. I didn't worry about what may be beneath Chapin's surface. None of us did. I am sure there was stuff that could kill us in there. That's the other side of potential. There are jagged rocks that could slice your foot or mud that could make you sink. It's the paradox of potential. We could tread water for hours then. But today, I haven't swum in years.

Scan any beach now and you'll see mostly children in the water. The adults will sit on shore. We like to be in environments we can regulate. Waves and wind have too much possibility for mishap. I can't remember the last time I left my house without checking my weather app. I keep a jacket in the back hatch of my car. It's called being responsible—a little trick I learned from my mother, who probably learned from hers. I would rather be anything than cold.

My beach runs now are survival guides in preparedness. Sunglasses, check. Sunblock, check. Cell phone, check. Ice, check. I bring a cooler. I don't want to drink anything that gets too warm. There is nothing worse than swallowing hot water on a warm day. Nothing worse than too hot or too cold. Nothing worse than chasing extremes. I adjust umbrellas and bring food to survive the two or three hours I will spend at the lake. I bring snacks to sit outside. Adults have to plan when they go outside. It's protection from the elements.

As a child, I sat my bottom right on the sand. I didn't have to think twice. This was living. Now I lug around chairs or lie on towels or pound stakes into the ground in an effort to make a tent. We may stay only an hour, and yet we bring with us something stable. We love to feel stable. Uncertainty is our greatest fear. Avoiding it becomes survival. Life—and feelings, dreams, and passions—must be controlled. Our desire for shelter is strong, even here. We turn nature into something more habitable. We want something between us and the stars. We want rafts for the water. We are afraid that if freedom presses up to our skin, we might lose ourselves chasing after it. And we are done with chasing.

Scripture describes Adam as being formed out of the dust of the earth, but adults don't like dust. Adam and Eve would be appalled. They'd never bring a cooler. We reject the very ground that we were metaphorically sculpted from. But even God gets in the dirt. The Lord was never afraid of mud. In Genesis 3:19 we see this illustration of God getting in the dirt to form Adam. And then again in Deuteronomy 34:5–7. He gets in the dirt to bury Moses.

John 9:6 says, "After saying this, [Jesus] spit on the ground, made some mud with the saliva, and put it on the man's eyes." Jesus pressed his hands into mud in order to make people clean.

Again, we find God in the dirt in John 8:8 when Jesus writes on the ground to stop the mob from stoning the woman caught in adultery. God gets in the dirt to form us, to heal us, to save us from our own sin, and even to bury us.

We, on the other hand, detest it. We sweep it. We vacuum it. In photos we angle the camera just right to make sure it stays out of view. We will scan our homes and cars for dirt, making sure we remove every speck. It reminds us of the ground we came from. It's a trigger. We have worked so hard to control our environments. We will do anything to make people believe that our lives are clean and tidy. That we have everything under control. That we are certain. You won't find any dirt beneath our fingernails. Passion doesn't pay for manicures. We won't even sit on a beach without a chair. Even in paradise, we need our regulators.

Tim Mackie makes an interesting note about the dirt we see in Genesis 2 and how it connects us back to the water.[2] Genesis 2:6–7 in the CSB reads, "But mist would come up from the earth and water all the ground. Then the LORD God formed the man out of the dust from the ground and breathed the breath of life into his nostrils, and the man became a living being."

Mackie explains that we will miss the connection in the English but that the poetry is more visible and audible in the Hebrew. The word for "mist" or "stream" used in verse 6 is *ed*. The Hebrew word for "man" is *adam*, and the Hebrew word for "ground" or "earth" is *adamah*. Mackie believes the biblical writer is doing wordplay in a culture that would orally share the Scriptures so that a Hebrew listener would quickly connect mist (*ed*) to the man (*adam*) and the earth (*adamah*). It brings a great symbolic beauty to Jesus, as God, creator of water and land, fully embodied and having water run from his side at the cross. Revelation 22:1 reads, "Then he showed me the river of the water of life, clear as crystal, flowing from the throne of God and of the Lamb" (CSB).

God will redeem all this dirt.

I had lunch with a friend yesterday. "I'm so unsure of everything," she said while eating chips and salsa. She is a mom of three who dared to dream enough to start her own business. But of course, building your dream is never easy. Work requires effort. Swimming will take your energy.

"And I don't even know what I am doing," she continued. "I'm having to work every shift to save money on employees. Heather, I don't even know if the business is going to work."

Remember, we are born with two basic fears. The fear of falling and the fear of loud noises. Everything else we learn to fear by experience. It takes great bravery for people to submit to a path of passion. It takes courage to face fear and decide to be unafraid. Very few adults will ever know it. In fact, we will sit with our chairs and our coolers and shout that everyone in the waves is a fool. To trade stability for suffering? To lose yourself in something that feels greater than your own comfort? My friend thought that she was drowning, but she was swimming.

I sat there with my manicure. Every finger trimmed. Nodding my head while she spoke. She was worried about finances. She was managing employees and conflict. It was a lot of mixed emotions. But there was something inspiring about her face. Something inviting even in her struggle. Something curious about her uncertainty. I was watching a woman who decided to believe that failing wasn't the worst thing that could happen to her. That dirt wasn't something to avoid. That perhaps all of these things were connected.

I was on the shore.

She was in the water.

> I am faint and severely crushed;
>> I groan because of the anguish of my heart.
>
> Psalm 38:8 CSB

DIVE DEEPER

1. What does Heather mean by "God gets in the dirt"?
2. After reading this chapter, what does water represent to you?
3. What risks might you be ready to take and in what areas of your life?

CHAPTER 8

PASSION PAINS

WHEN I WAS A FRESHMAN IN HIGH SCHOOL, MY dad told me to get in the passenger seat.

"Where are we going?" I asked him while loading myself into the boat that was his Lincoln Town Car.

"We are investing in your future," he said.

He drove me no more than three miles. My future was apparently close to the house. It was the university in our town. Dad was beaming as he parked the car and handed me a notebook. The campus building we walked into was made of old stone. The door was wood and glass and it was almost too heavy to open. The inside smelled like dust and pages. Dad skipped down the hallway and looked at the plaques on the wall that labeled each department.

"English," he said out loud, tapping the sign with his pointer finger. He turned the doorknob that would then lead us to several offices. Again, he inspected the plaques on the wall until his pointer finger reemerged. He tapped the nameplate and smiled at me.

"This is it," he said. "I'll be back for you in an hour."

"What am I doing here?" I asked him as he lifted his palm to tap on the large wooden door.

"Writing," he whispered.

My dad had paid a university professor to do writing exercises with me that summer. She gave me story prompts and I'd imagine new worlds and then bring them for her to evaluate the next week. Week after week, while other kids enjoyed their summer, Dad would drive me in the boat and then push me out to sea. I honestly hated those writing classes. I would have rather been at Lake Chapin. But they also gave me something that, more than twenty years later, I can still close my eyes and see. A memory of my dad believing in me.

I was twenty-five the first time my passion crushed me beneath it. It always starts with childhood, doesn't it? If you follow that line long enough, you'll connect the dots to the last time you felt free. I have diaries and journals littered with dreams that drowned. I suffocated them. That's how you kill something. You stop giving it so much oxygen. You drag it to the depths of the sea. You don't come up for air. You leave it in darkness and stop looking for shafts of light. You learn to hide what becomes painful. The interesting thing about dreams is that no one else can kill them. People can hurt them or delay them. Outsiders can laugh at them. But they are like an anchor with weight so heavy no one else can lift it. In order to destroy a dream completely, it is only your hand that can pull the rope that has kept your boat from sailing.

It always starts with childhood. All I wanted as a child was to write books. Every time I mention writing in this book, please insert your passion in place of mine. I am only using myself as a safe example. It's like share time in group therapy. I tell you a little about my story, but you connect the dots to your own. This story is about you as much as it's about me. And I hope we both are lighter for sharing.

From the time I was old enough to hold a pen, I wrote. How old were you the first time you held yours? Whatever "yours" means. Maybe it was ministry or dance. Maybe it was music or content creation, business, medicine, technology, law, politics, or romance, whatever that space is that made you stand a little taller. This is, of course, before it crushed you beneath it. Not because you didn't believe but because of how much of yourself you gave to it. Where did all that giving get you?

As a kid we feel like we can be a little piece of everything. We can be an astronaut and an actor. A fireman and a teacher. Each piece complemented the other. But as adults we try hard to focus in. Shave the subpoints. Trim the fat. Narrow our focus because all the pieces can't fit. Something must be lost. And maybe that something becomes us. At some point in adulthood, we decide you can be only one thing, and you have to be paid for it, and you have to be better than everyone else or it doesn't count. A passion without the ability for comparison or monetization is just a silly hobby. Cute, but get a real job.

And so, if we can't bow the head of our dreams to the graven image of capitalism, we feel like we have failed. Why would I write for free? Why would I make something without applause? The symbol of success is a dollar sign. Rich and righteous Christians find value in what is received over what is given. What do you do with a doctor who can't pass med school? What does a lawyer become when they can't pass the bar? Our dreams were to be paid to do what we loved. Eventually we decide that being numb would be safer than dreaming. That rejection and pain is too great a cost. Throw down the anchor; get me out of the water. Keep these wings away from the sun.

Remember, *passion* literally means "to suffer." We say we want a life of passion, but we really want a life of affirmation. Passion isn't about what we do for applause. It's about what we can't stop doing, even without it. What do you love so much you'd be willing to face the pain of losing it over and over again? For a lot of us, the answer is, "Nothing." And so we go through life feeling nothing.

I told everyone I was a writer. I didn't mean it as a job. It was who I was. With or without a paycheck. I didn't need money back then to prove anything. My dream itself was enough. They'd see. What were you before you needed someone else to confirm it? It wasn't even that it made you happy to do it as much as it was simply a part of who you were. It wasn't something you did. It was a means by which you became better able to be who you already were. It made you feel free. And wild. You'd get in the dirt with it. You'd jump off the pier. No matter how cold things got, this was part of what made you feel warm. It was an internal thermometer. Your thermostat. You didn't need a weather app.

Do you remember when holding dreams felt easy? Before all the triggers and baggage? Before all the disappointments and wounds? Before degrees and paychecks? Before marriages and divorces? Before "single" became a mental category? Before children and empty nesting? Before responsibility made everything heavy? Before the world shouted back that you couldn't just "be" things without an official title or a way to prove how much better you are than everyone else who does it? We learn in adulthood that we don't get to know who we are in and of ourselves. Not unless we get permission. The committee must meet. There needs to be a unanimous decision. Who sat on that board for you? Who told you who you were good enough for you to believe it?

For me, the dream had always been writing. I'd go back to that first time I ever lifted a pen if I could. The first time I ever heard ink scratch across paper. I wrote the following line in my first book. I can still remember it. I can still hear my voice, raspy and delighted, reading it aloud in my room, and then to my parents. They were on my committee. They helped me jump into the water. They never told me to drop an anchor. I did that on my own.

"A pen is an instrument. It's a writer's piano. In the wrong hands, it can make an awful pitch. But in the hands of a skilled musician, you can almost hear music playing." I wrote and I wrote and I did it for free.

My childhood was filled with melodies. My fantasies grew with each word. Words expand, you know. Not just on pages but also in our minds. Words are not just letters standing side by side. They are dreams. They are visions. They are thoughts and ideas that spiral us both up and down hills. Words create our sincerest passion, and yet words can cause our deepest pain. They take shape and then take up space in our lives. It's fascinating, really. How at first we create them and then we become them. They expand. Words create our reality.

Words are powerful. Which is why I'll string them delicately on this very line. It is why you must be gentle with yourself as you let your lips release their syllables. Be careful, little mouth, what you say; your brain is actually listening to you. The Word of God is filled with examples of what words can do.

The Bible, which is honestly more of a library, is made up of 43 percent narrative and 33 percent song and poetry. This makes up 76 percent of our Bible.[1] The remaining 24 percent is prose, which includes things like essays and speeches. No one told me, though, that being a good Bible student would also mean being a good student of story and poetry and literary devices. No one told me that just reading the Bible wasn't studying the Bible. That there was context to the words on the page and cultural components I couldn't understand just by reading it. As a communications professor, context naturally fascinates me. Context always changes the conversation. I have spent a great deal of time just thinking about the implications of 76 percent of our Bible being story, song, and poetry. It requires of us much deeper reflection than just reading.

Because of this, and my fascination with how Jesus so often used parables to explain important religious teachings, I wrote my dissertation on storytelling. It was surely a pursuit of passion. For five years I struggled through my PhD program, where I researched and read and analyzed the significance of storytelling in building relationship. Did you know that we remember stories up to twenty-two times better than facts alone?[2] Or that our brains can't help but place ourselves cognitively inside a story when we hear one? We experience stories as if they are really happening to us. This is why we jump when we're watching a scary movie, though the monster is on the screen and not in our room. Stories become part of who we are. Reading, listening, and sharing our stories with others is an incredibly transformative experience. You can take people to where only you have been by sharing with them your story.

I was twenty-five the first time my own story of passion started to crush me. Writing became suffering that same year. It went from something I did to express myself to something that had sales numbers and rejection letters attached to it. It also felt like I was perpetually failing my dad.

When I was twenty-five, my dad's diagnosis had come in, and the wave of grief knocked me over. I haven't really stood since. He was the person who invested in my future. He believed in me, which became shame when I no longer believed in myself. Because I saw so much of myself in my dad, his Alzheimer's frightened me. He deserved better than that. It became difficult for me to believe in the dream of writing when my dad couldn't remember the words. He was always my greatest supporter.

"You are going to be something, Heather," he used to tell me when I came home from school in tears. I was not an easy kid to raise. I was expelled from my Christian middle school a year before my dad bought me the writing lessons. My principal literally looked me in the eyes and told me, "Sometimes one bad peach can spoil the whole crate."

It's a core wound that has driven a lot of my choices. I embarrassed my parents as a child, so I would make them proud as an adult. My dad never once acted embarrassed of me. He said that small church schools didn't know how to handle leaders when they were girls. He said that I had a gift for writing. And when he got Alzheimer's, it was hard for me to remember if any of that was true without his voice there to repeat it. Words create our reality. As do the lack of them.

"What's my name?" I asked, cornering my dad this past July. I had noticed he had stopped saying it. I was scared to find out why.

"Don't be silly," he said, smiling.

I told you my dad was an actor. He is very good, even with his disease, at hiding what he doesn't know. When people from his past see him and act like they know him, he acts too. If you talk to him for only a couple of minutes, you may not notice he has no clue who you are. This can also backfire. If a stranger he has never met does even a Midwestern wave, he will rush right over and call them "buddy" and ask how they've been. They will have no clue who he is, and he has no clue who they are, but now both of them are trapped in this dialogue, waiting to see who breaks first.

"Dad," I said with tears in my eyes. "It's okay if you don't know. I won't be mad."

I was whispering because I didn't want my mom, sister, or brother to hear. I would let him perform for them a little longer.

"I . . . don't . . . know . . ." his voice trailed off and he mouthed something but never made a sound.

I think he was trying to recall the word *names*.

"I don't know names" is what I think he wanted to say, but I'll never know. His face fell and he looked defeated. Embarrassment flashed across his eyes.

"I . . . don't . . . know . . ." he began again, still not finding whatever word he was looking for.

"But I know you." He locked his gaze with mine. It was a look he used to give me when his mind was healthy. A look of deep knowing. He would do it when he wanted to make sure I understood something complicated. I hadn't seen that look in years.

His face was no longer defeated. His eyes held no shame. In fact, he looked proud. Proud that he knew me. It was all that I ever wanted. It was balm to my old eighth-grade wounds. I hugged him tight, and he melted in my arms. He had held me as a child, but I was holding him now. My dad gave me something this past July that is a gift only Alzheimer's could give me. It's a bittersweet understanding. A fresh perspective you get only when you come face-to-face with a wave that's bigger and stronger than you are. A wave that breaks you and then forms you. A passion so strong it lifts every anchor.

My own dad didn't know my name anymore. But the bond between us was bigger than that. It could not be defined by terms.

But I know you, he had said. And that day I decided that I needed to know me too.

I picked up a pen and started writing. It didn't matter if it was published. It didn't matter if it was ever read. It didn't matter if people knew my name.

I put on my wings and got off the shore. I was heading for the sun.

> Whatever you do, do it from the heart, as something done for the Lord and not for people.
>
> Colossians 3:23 CSB

DIVE DEEPER

1. Thinking about the true definition of *passion*, what are you passionate about?
2. Who has always been on your "committee"—whose approval have you always sought?
3. If you weren't afraid you would fail, what would you do?

CHAPTER 9

MEET ME AT THE FOUNTAIN

WHEN NFL STAR TRAVIS KELCE WAS A YOUNG man, his college football coach offered him some words of wisdom.

"Everybody you meet in this world is either a fountain or a drain . . . I need fountains."[1]

In a world where so much about our lives can feel so draining, the idea that one could still choose to be a fountain deeply resonated with me. I have never been more spiritually convicted by a *Wall Street Journal* article about a football player.

By thirty-two I had come to realize that whether I was a fountain that provided cool springs for others had almost nothing to do with whether I attained my dreams. Not until I was thirty-six would I start asking myself an even bigger question than what my dreams are. I started to ask myself what my passion is. And again, when I say *passion*, I am using the word in its biblical definition. You'll remember that *passion*, biblically, means "to suffer." Of course, I knew already what

I loved. But I didn't consciously understand that passion was deeper than that. That it would be both what I loved and what I loved enough to suffer for or through. Also, by thirty-six, I had stopped seeing suffering as something that I needed to avoid at all costs. I had several years of therapy under my belt and was no longer numbing myself with work. I was feeling all of my life. The good, the bad, and the beautiful. By this point, I had rejected the lessons of Icarus. I knew that going too low could never be avoided. It was the consequence of being willing to fly high. I had paid my therapist enough copays to accept that suffering didn't mean I had done anything wrong. Suffering just is. I had also walked with the Lord enough to see God differently. By thirty-six, I understood that I was never more connected to Christ than when I knew love, and I also felt that connection to humanity in suffering. The passion of Christ was the covenantal work of Jesus as Creator.

What was I so passionate about that I was willing to suffer for and through it? What was something that meant so much to me, in a world of drains, that I could still produce a fountain? What was so beautiful and precious and invigorating to my life that it left me willing to get too close to the sun? What do you love so much that suffering for it sounds more desirable than living without it? Or than living numb?

Becoming a professor for me was option B. Option A, to become a *New York Times* bestselling author, felt like a fool's errand. By the time I was twenty-five and watching my hero slowly die of Alzheimer's, I had decided that financial security was better than suffering. Dreams started to look too risky, so

I entered a college classroom again—this time as the teacher. I had published one book at that point with a really small church publisher that is now out of business. I found a copy of that book in my basement a couple of months ago. I opened it and found myself immediately stunned at how much I had changed since writing it over a decade ago.

My theology was different. My writing style was different. It was filled with typical Christian tropes that now I can hardly stomach. I always tell people not to read anything I published before 2016. I laughed to myself at how grateful I am that more people didn't buy that book when it was still in print. I realized that day in my basement that my passion wasn't really producing books. Books are wonderful, but I will outgrow them. If I'm lucky, and I am growing, learning, and continuing to develop as a human being, the words I print on a page will simply serve as markers of that journey. It took me reading my first book again ten years later to realize that books weren't necessarily my passion. It's the process of writing, the quietness of it, the research that goes into it, the spiritual component it gives me. It's the methodical way writers try to capture ideas and transcribe them so we can spark similar and even deeper ideas in others—that really moves me. Do you know what I would do now even if I never sold another book? I would keep writing. Because a pen, for me, is a fountain.

I started writing a Friday night newsletter I called *Friday Night Light*. It's filled with short, encouraging thoughts that will hopefully inspire you to pray through discouragement. I send it out every Friday night at 7:00 p.m. Eastern Standard

Time. (You can subscribe by going to HeatherThompsonDay.com.) It's my smallest community. I don't get paid for it; in fact, it costs me money. And yet I pray all week about what I will send out on Fridays to encourage a community of about six thousand people. It is probably one of my favorite moments each week. Sitting down at my computer and drafting that newsletter. I don't need a committee to do it. I don't need an agent or a publishing house or a marketing team. I don't need permission or a *New York Times* accolade to do what I believe God has called me to do: encourage people through writing. You don't need permission either.

Maybe you have a dream to publish a book. Are you compelled to challenge, encourage, prompt, or inspire people through writing? Why are you waiting on a book deal to give you permission to do it? If that comes, great, but don't spend your life waiting for permission to do what God has called you to. In fact, I believe it is possible that what God is calling you to may be outside the scope of what you can even fathom right now. So much will come in the unfolding of your life that you can't even perceive. Some of us will experience our best years at sixty. You may really hit your stride in your seventies. So much more living is ahead of you, and it is possible that it will take you places you can't grasp from sitting where you are today.

Is your dream to be a surgeon? Or is your dream to help improve health outcomes through medicine? Is there another avenue that allows you to meet that same objective? If life doesn't give you option A, what rerouting can you do to find effective ways to still pursue option B? If med school doesn't work out, does that mean that you can't still pursue your actual passion of helping people through health care? And maybe it won't give you the same amount of glory as the title "surgeon" will, but what if passion was never about glory at all? And what if God can actually do *more* through you in your option B than he could have done with your option A? What if God doesn't need your plans at all? What if the death of our dreams can be the birth of our passions?

Our passion isn't found in titles. The very definition of the word itself means that it can't be. Passion means "to suffer." What if passion is found only in showing up and doing the work we feel we have been called to without people affirming us for it? What do you feel called to so deeply that it's bigger than the accolades or the financial implications or the prestige? The work itself brings out a fountain within you that compels you to do it despite all those things rather than because of them.

Does a musician need a record label in order to bless others with music? What makes an artist an artist? Or a creator a creator? What makes a ministry a ministry? And who decides? Is it what we produce or who consumes it? My entire world flipped upside down that July when my own dad didn't know my name yet told me that he did know who I was. Because I realized that I have to know what makes me, me, outside of names and titles. Who all of us are is so much bigger than a label. It is my belief that our persistence in producing our gifts *despite* whatever challenges and obstacles we encounter is where the term *passion* is most correctly applied. Else we aren't pursuing our passion; we are pursuing a title. Or fame. Or financial reward.

Or prestige. Or followers on social media. Or big houses and fancy cars. And that is fine. I don't think those things are bad, but I think the way we use language helps our brains bring the truth of our relationship to those words into focus.

Are you passionate about medicine or are you passionate about money? This distinction matters because there are ways for you to still achieve financial security without being a doctor. But your brain can't even go there if you aren't first honest with yourself about where your heart is. Are you passionate about ministry or are you passionate about crowds? There is a distinction here that is incredibly important. You can have crowds and be a corporate speaker. I am not being dismissive when I say this. It is so important that we be honest with ourselves about what we really want. Because when we aren't, we get stuck in things we don't actually feel called to. We expend energy chasing what we have called our passion, but truly it is something else.

The crowd is in no way the barometer of your anointing. Your anointing is in *how* you walk out your calling faithfully. Are you passionate about writing or are you passionate about bestseller lists? Being honest about where our passion truly lies is key to understanding ourselves.

I am not saying you have to abandon financial stability. I am not saying that we must pursue poverty and insignificance to be noble. But I am saying that money will not make you who you are. Neither will a title or accolade. The problem with hustle culture is that it has caused us to believe that the only passions worth having are the ones we can profit from. In my humble opinion, this mindset negates the very meaning of *passion*. If your life is feeling numb or drained or unfulfilling, I think it's possible that it's because you have stopped tapping into your inner fountain. In today's culture, we don't see value in things that aren't somehow going to lead us to bigger and better opportunities. But I think this is one of the dangers of capitalism. It has us thinking about how to mine our giftings to make a profit for ourselves rather than how to use our giftings to profit others. This is especially dangerous territory for the Christian.

Since my passion was always writing, and my writing career wasn't taking off, I ended up looking for an opportunity in my option B. Being a professor would allow me to write lectures and maybe textbooks. It would allow me to have summers off where I could write if the opportunity ever arose. Teaching would give me the ability to do for others what I felt like I couldn't do for myself anymore: inspire them to swim. From my very first day teaching, I spent an exceptional amount of time writing. I didn't just get up and teach; I wrote down lectures for myself almost word for word. I spent a great deal of energy trying to figure out how to teach a concept in such a way that students would feel it held personal application to their lives. I didn't want to just be a teacher. I wanted to bring living water to dry ground.

I want you to take some time and think about option B. I know that very phrase may make you want to sob. And I would say, don't resist that urge. My brain was stuck for a long time on how things in my life were supposed to play out. But can I tell you the hand-to-heart truth? Teaching *is* my gift. Possibly even more clearly visible than writing is. But I had no idea because anything other than writing, in my limited perspective at that time, felt like failure. Today, I truly think that what I thought was option B was actually God's option A; he was just waiting for me to trust him enough to follow him where he was going rather than demand that he follow me where I was going.

I want you to zoom out. Take a few days or weeks or months and ask yourself a very important question: Why?

Why do you want to be a lawyer? Why do you want to be a surgeon? Why do you want to have a business? And who are you if none of those titles ever gets applied to your name? Ruth Bader Ginsburg was a brilliant law scholar. She was enrolled in Harvard Law School from 1956 to 1958.[2] She was even editor of the *Harvard Law Review*. She ended up transferring to Columbia, where she graduated first in her class. But then, due to her gender and the fact that it was the sixties, she couldn't get hired as a lawyer. But Ginsburg was *passionate* about the law. I am using that word correctly. The legal system was something she was willing to suffer through. Option A was to be a lawyer, but when that didn't work, she secured a job as a law clerk. Later, she became a professor at Rutgers Law School, teaching civil procedures. She spent most of her career as an advocate for gender equality and women's rights. She was nominated in 1993 as the first Jewish woman to serve on the Supreme Court. Ginsburg kept doing what she loved, even without a title, even without prestige, even without accolades. And the world noticed. What if Ginsburg had stopped trying to pursue a law career after her setbacks in her youth?

Option B doesn't mean that option A won't happen. It doesn't mean that you are giving up. It doesn't mean that you are a quitter. It's actually the opposite. Option B is called *resilience*. My intentionality in how I prepared lectures is actually what got my feet back into the water. I realized that I didn't need the *New York Times* to validate a piece of me that I already owned. I was going to partake in my passion with or without them. And I noticed over several years and many classroom lectures later that when you use your passion in service to others, it really does serve them as much as it serves you.

What is your option B? What step moves you forward, even if in the moment it feels like failure? In what aspect can you use pieces of your original dream to serve you in practical ways right now?

I served at a homeless shelter for many years. When I say that, you may think I mean in the soup kitchen or handing out blankets. But I don't. I taught a class there and wrote lectures on self-awareness and self-concept and communication. I had countless incredible interactions with people I met there over the years. I absolutely loved volunteering my time and trying to figure out how to take lessons I had written for eighteen-year-old students and turn them into concepts that could inspire people of all different ages and backgrounds. It changed my life. It changed my communication. It changed the way I saw people. Teaching was not even on my radar in undergrad, and yet today, these experiences have deeply shaped who I am.

Today, one of my main forms of ministry is teaching. But I didn't know that back then. I had no idea this was even in my gifting. That wasn't in my option A. That piece of my ministry was birthed only out of option B. The greatest ministry I have today was something I discovered only because I couldn't reach my dream. It is a gifting I learned while showing up to the homeless shelter. It is a passion I developed while being faithful in my classroom to sometimes as few as three students. If you would have told me while I was making $49,000 a year at a community college or teaching a class of three at the homeless shelter that God was actually honing and sharpening my skills to speak in front of thousands, I would have asked you a million follow-up questions.

The first of which would have been, "But do I have a *New York Times* bestseller?"

And then you would have had to tell me, "No."

That option A hasn't happened. But you can gain something greater than numbers can reveal. You can become a person who knows who you are without anyone there to tell you.

And God can release a fountain when you release your plans.

"Woe to the rebellious children!
　　This is the LORD's declaration.
　　They carry out a plan, but not mine."

Isaiah 30:1 CSB

DIVE DEEPER

1. Who are you? Don't say a job title.
2. What may be some paths toward option B for you?
3. How can you be a fountain right now?

CHAPTER 10

GOD KEEPS SCORE

I USED TO WATCH MY DAD WRITING SONGS IN the dungeon. He would go down there for hours and come back up with an entire set list or show or script. I would sneak down about four steps and peer under the railing. He wouldn't even notice I was there. Not when he was in his creative headspace. The entire world vanished, and only the one he was creating emerged. I always felt bad that I couldn't sing. None of my siblings can. Music was such a big part of my dad's life. He taught himself how to play piano and guitar. He could play any song by ear.

I brought him to my house the other day. He can no longer be home alone. He was becoming anxious and agitated, as Alzheimer's patients often do. It's a part of him that I have never known. I grabbed my phone and played "Midnight Cry," a song written by Greg Day. When Greg was seven, a preacher called him up to the front of his church and said, "One day when you are older . . . you will write a song that will change lives."[1]

In 1986 Greg and his brother were visiting their parents' church in Georgia during an evangelistic series. The sermon was called "Midnight Cry," and when Greg heard it, he wrote the title on a business card. That afternoon, while playing a few notes on a piano, Greg sang, "I hear the sound of a mighty rushing wind," and his brother, without missing a beat, responded, "and it's closer now than it has ever been." It would take them exactly thirty minutes to write that song. A song I would hear my dad sing in the hallways of my home my entire life. He sang it at almost every church he brought his ministry to, and tears would flood the room. I have never in my life heard anyone sing "Midnight Cry" with the passion that my dad gave it. His only brother, Jonathan Thompson, died a few years into my dad's diagnosis. My dad was forgetful then but still had a resemblance to the man I had always known. His sisters asked if he could still sing, and sing he did. My uncle's funeral was filled with mourning people who all left with hope in their hearts after my dad's version of "Midnight Cry."

So when Dad got distressed in my home, I decided to play it. He didn't know my name anymore, but as I played the song on my phone, his agitated face immediately brightened. Without having to even think, his voice boomed across my hallway like it did when I was a kid.

"I hear the sound," he sang, "of a mighty rushing wind." I turned on my phone's camera and started to record him. "And it's closer now," he began to raise his arms, "than it has ever been."

He still had the skill of a professional vocalist. My dad couldn't hold a conversation, but he could still sing. That preacher who spoke to seven-year-old Greg Day was right. He would write a song that would change lives. Dad sang the song over and over probably six times. He stopped only because I worried his voice would get hoarse, so I turned it off. Every word dancing out of his mouth surrounded my home in the echoes of my childhood. That beautiful vibrato. I discovered that afternoon that there was something inside my dad that even Alzheimer's couldn't take away: his passion.

I often think about how watching my father influenced me, and I am keenly aware of how my own passion was inherited by my daughter. She will spend hours writing stories in her room. She uses a real pen, just like I did at her age. Sometimes families provide us with little direction toward our dreams and passions, and other times they pass passions down like heirlooms. Stories are always shaping us. And for many of us, we aren't just born into a family; we are born into an already developing story arc.

A mom who was a teacher, and so now you are a teacher. A dad who was a doctor, and so now you are a doctor. A grandmother who couldn't afford to go to college, and a granddaughter who secures a full-ride scholarship. I am often fascinated by how stories end up interweaving themselves generationally. For many families they are heirlooms. Some that we couldn't get to fit and others that we wished we could afford.

Is it coincidence that Taylor Swift's grandmother was an opera singer? Jim Carrey said that his father had wanted to be a comedian but didn't think it was a safe choice. He needed to pay bills. Raise kids. Make conservative choices. He became an accountant.

Carrey, who of course became a very successful comedian, said, "When I was 12 years old, he [Dad] was let go from that safe job. . . . Our family had to do whatever we could to survive. I learned many great lessons from my father, not the least of which is that you can fail at what you don't want, so you might as well take a chance on doing what you love."[2]

My path never really felt like it was just about me. I am not sure if this is normal or something that happens a lot in minority families. My parents' dreams come with me everywhere. Every failure always felt multiplied for me because I didn't just feel like I was failing myself; I felt like I was failing them. And as I told you earlier, when you do something that you fear shames your family, like getting expelled from your eighth-grade church school, you either continue down that path or become determined to leave it. I became obsessed with making my parents proud. When you don't grow up into inherited wealth but into hardworking families that give up a lot just to pay your school bill, you are extremely aware that every class you take has cost them something.

Many years ago I had a Korean boss. He had changed his job a few times. He was brilliant and artistic and actually became a filmmaker. But he became a filmmaker later in life. His first job was in medicine. He was a physical therapist. I asked him one day why he would get a doctorate in physical therapy when he was so clearly gifted in film.

"Immigrants often don't get to pursue the arts," he said. "It's too risky. Your parents gave up too much. Physical therapy was the only way I knew for sure I could repay them."

I knew, to a lesser degree, what he was talking about. I knew the weight of trying to validate your parents' investments in you. I knew the responsibility of carrying their dreams. I think a lot of us do. Sometimes I wonder if my daughter loves writing or if she really loves her mom. Those lines can get blurry for some of us as children. When we see our parents work hard to achieve something, we can't help but see ourselves within that story. Because that's what stories do. They swallow everything around them.

When I was eleven, I had one childhood prayer that God never answered. I would pray it on repeat:

"Dear Jesus, please just let me be an author."

I had countless diaries and journals. I wrote stories and poetry between classes. I was fifteen years old, pitching manuscripts to agents. I would google publishing houses and send them book proposals. Very few people ever wrote me back.

I would cry most years on my birthday. Once I was alone in my room, I would thank God for my family, and friends, and gifts, but I would tell him, "I want to be an author. Don't you remember?"

Over two decades have passed since I was eleven. I never did become a child author. But you want to know something so bizarre I have a feeling it may stir up something deep within you? A few months ago, my daughter and I signed a publishing contract for a children's book. It's called *Can I Sit Here?* and tells her story of being excluded. We wrote it together. It's the story of her sitting down at a lunch table in third grade and having every other girl sitting there get up and move their trays.

My daughter couldn't be happier about the opportunity to share her experience of being bullied with other kids and help them feel less alone.

To be honest, I am not sure my daughter has ever prayed a single prayer about being an author. She's a fantastic writer. But I am not sure she even knew kids could do something like that. Do you want to know how old my daughter was at the time of her contract? She was eleven.

Every night from the time I was eleven, I asked God to allow me to be an author. For over two decades, I thought those prayers simply went unanswered or were delayed into my adulthood. They expired. But when we signed a book contract, I was overwhelmed with an intense feeling of the Holy Spirit, and the Lord revealed something so powerful that it literally knocked the wind out of me. *God remembered.*

Many times in the Old Testament, God references one of Israel's predecessors that God was still honoring, even hundreds of years later. We see it in Jeremiah 15:1, where the Bible says, "Then the LORD said to me: 'Even if Moses and Samuel were to stand before me, my heart would not go out to this people.'"

For God to say this might also mean that in general, the opposite is also true. That the prayers of Israel's ancestors were often what was protecting them in their present state. For example, Malachi 3:6 says, "I am the LORD, and I do not change. That is why you descendants of Jacob are not already destroyed" (NLT). And 2 Kings 13:23 reads, "The LORD was gracious to them, had compassion on them, and turned toward them because of his covenant with Abraham, Isaac, and Jacob" (CSB).

The Bible is a connected family story, as are our lives. I don't believe you are reading this book by accident. And it's probably not a coincidence that you are still wrestling through your spiritual life and seeking God's guidance and encouragement. Do you think it's by chance that you are still seeking, still praying, still calling out to God? It would have been much easier for you to quit than to continue in this passionate suffering. What if there are prayers that have gone before you? What if the only reason I am writing this is because my nana prayed that God would use her children, and that prayer extends to me? What if I am not here on my own but I am walking in the legacy of prayers prayed on my behalf a hundred years before I was even born?

Your life is more beautiful and precious and providential than you can even dream! Think about meeting your ancestors in heaven whose prayers went before you. Men and women of great faith whom God knew and called by name. And what if, just maybe, your prayers today are a part of what will protect and encourage future generations, long after you and I are both gone?

When I go on prayer walks, I often ask God to honor, through my life, the prayers that came before me. I don't always know what to pray, and so sometimes I wonder if my great-great-grandmother already has. I remember Ezekiel 14:14 and 2 Kings 13:23 and that we are all connected. That truly, we are a part of this vast global family, and as separate as we think our lives may be, we are often receiving an inheritance we didn't earn. I don't think our dreams expire the way we think they do. I think God remembers. Even if your family ten generations back was not religious, as a Christian, you are now grafted into the covenant of a new family. You are surely walking in the prayers of Noah, Daniel, and Paul. The cries of Moses and Samuel. The songs of Ruth and Naomi. The prayers of Mary. The petition, in the garden of Gethsemane, of Jesus, the one who they called Christ. You are never alone.

I know so many people who talk about the sins of their parents and grandparents as if those sins will keep them bound throughout their own lives. And truly, the Bible does say in Deuteronomy that we will be breaking generational curses up to the third and fourth generation (Deuteronomy 5:9). But God also says in Deuteronomy 7:9 that God keeps his gracious covenant for a thousand generations. That is how God does math. In your favor, not your debt. And so I want you to remember that there are surely prayers over your life that have long preceded you. And the good news of the gospel is that God has kept and will continue to keep his promises. Second Corinthians 1:20 reads, "No matter how many promises God has made, they are 'Yes' in Christ. And so through him the 'Amen' is spoken by us to the glory of God."

It is a lie to think you are sitting or standing wherever you are right now on your own. Prayers have gone before you. You are a part of the family of God. It is "our father, who art in heaven. . . ." Christianity is a community that you belong to. And the decisions you make and the prayers you pray today will not expire upon your death. They will ascend to the throne of God over your children and their children, long after you have stopped praying them. We are all connected through Christ.

I truly believe my daughter, throughout her life, is going to reap blessings she didn't even know to pray for. And as I sit with you right now, I have a deep sense that I am walking in the prayers my father prayed before me. I wonder if my great-grandmother wrote in journals prayers that I will never read. I wonder if my great-great-grandfather wanted to do ministry. I wonder who of my ancestors prayed prayers that they went to their graves thinking God never heard. But God remembered.

I won't pretend to know exactly how prayer works. I'm not sure why some of our prayers get delayed. I don't know why some of us will go to our graves thinking God didn't hear a word we said. All I know is that my daughter got her first publishing contract at the exact same age I first asked God for my own. And it has me wondering if we are a part of something much bigger and more connected than we even understand.

You may think your dreams and passions burning within began with you. But what if they didn't? What if all of us are a part of a story that is much bigger than ourselves? What if prayers don't expire? What if your path isn't meaningless? What if angels are working connecting dots that span multiple generations?

I've been thinking about how many people my dad has forgotten. How many memories he has lost. How many anniversaries and dates and birthdays no longer exist in his mind. And I think something interesting happens to our memories when losing people we've loved a lot.

We become consumed by remembering.

Then God remembered Rachel and answered her prayer.

Genesis 30:22 NCV

DIVE DEEPER

1. What does Heather mean when she asks, "What if our prayers don't expire?"
2. Are there any similar patterns in your family when it comes to your passion?
3. What is a prayer that God may be answering in your life that past generations could have actually prayed?

CHAPTER 11

THE WELL

I SET UP A MEETING WITH SOMEONE AT WORK who was many steps my senior. They outranked me in pay and position. It is not my normal nature to shake the apple cart, but I needed to lodge a complaint. I like to keep my head down and do my job. I'm wind that blows through my campus halls. You don't know when I came or in which direction I left. I am relatively silent in faculty meetings. I don't complain or feel the need to insert my opinion unless someone asks. Teaching for me has always been about my students. I give them 110 percent of my attention and energy. The meetings and policy and interdepartmental scurry don't pique my interest. And yet here I was, setting up a meeting with someone as high up the command chain as one can go. It was my first, albeit necessary, trip to the executive suite.

What got me to walk up those three flights of stairs wasn't a policy but a person. A coworker whom I had watched give her heart to our campus was having her position eliminated. She was an immigrant, single, Black woman, striking almost every box on the quartet of the vulnerable that Scripture commands us to care for: immigrants, widows, orphans, and the poor. I genuinely believe every Christian should be conscious of these four groups at all times. Who do you know who fits in one of these categories, and in what ways can you provide support when you are able? Of course, widowhood in Scripture is much more than just a woman who has lost her husband. I think the same is true of orphans. Students on my campus who don't have adult involvement in their lives are socially orphaned. Or international students who are unable to receive support from their families and are socially bereft of the support adult intervention can offer. It is important for me, as I live out Scripture's counsel, to pay attention to these groups and support them as best as I am able. Widowhood is more than just women whose husbands have died.

I watched a sermon by K. A. Ellis once where she explained that the word for widow in Scripture is *hera*, which means "bereft."[1] In the biblical context, a woman who is without the social and cultural agency of a man or a family is a widow. This should cause you to rethink how we treat single women in our church communities. How are we supporting them? How are we coming alongside them? How are we carrying burdens with them? My coworker was *hera*, a widow.

My friend, however, was much more than a bereft widow in need of my aid. She had, on multiple occasions, come alongside and supported me. She had recommended books to me that she thought would enhance my theology. She had walked the beach with me and listened to my dreams. She had bought me lunch on more than one occasion and prayed with me when I confided in her what was happening with my dad. As is often the blessing of Christian community, there was a mutuality to our relationship that sharpened us both.

I was on my knees praying for her one morning at five o'clock, and I felt very clearly that I was supposed to schedule a meeting. I needed to speak truth to power. I needed to advocate for someone who was worthy of it. I didn't know how this was going to go. Powerful people rarely like to be confronted by people with very little power, but I was going to be obedient to what I felt God calling me into, which was accountability on my coworker's behalf. I wasn't sure what repercussions would come from my conversation with my employer, but passion rarely focuses on things like that.

I had a student once who lost her mother midsemester. When I asked her how she was doing, she said that she would have dropped out had this particular coworker not supported her both emotionally and financially. Some people get applause for doing the bare minimum. This woman I worked with was giving of every resource she had, but because she served quietly, many weren't aware of her contributions. Now she was losing her job at Christmastime. I won't get into the politics of it, though you can be assured the reasons for her position being cut were political. I was sick over what was happening to such a faithful person.

As I entered the administration building, I had no idea what I was going to say when I got to the top of the stairs, but I was suddenly extremely thirsty. *Maybe vulnerability can cause your throat to get dry*, I thought. I know it's a very common symptom of anxiety. When I reached the top of the flight, I asked God to give me the right words to speak on another person's behalf. Once inside the office of the senior official, I began, so calmly that honestly it shocked me, to share what was on my heart.

"I believe you have valued politics over the person," I said.

"Excuse me," they coughed, after struggling a bit in their response. Next thing I knew they walked over to their desk and reached for a bottle of water. I had been in their office for no more than ten minutes. And in that period, I watched them grasp for water three times. Vulnerability *can* cause your throat to get dry. We have to be willing as Christians to place ourselves in vulnerable positions for others. We have to be willing to walk up several flights of stairs. To advocate for the Christian vision of community. Christianity is a religion that propels us not only to serve the vulnerable but to become vulnerable for the sake of others.

Isaiah 41:17–18 makes a connection to water and vulnerability. It reads,

The poor and the needy seek water, but there is none; their tongues are parched with thirst. I will answer them. I am the LORD, the God of Israel. I will not abandon them. I will open rivers on the barren heights, and springs in the middle of the plains. I will turn the desert into a pool and dry land into springs. (CSB)

Water is an extremely important resource anywhere, but particularly in the desert. Without it, fairly quickly, we all die.

The story in John 4 of the woman at the well has always fascinated me. It is one of the stories where we get to see the heavenly power that rested on Jesus but also his frailty as a human being. He is thirsty. And honestly, I can't get over it. A King who leaves his throne. A God who exits heaven to enter earth. Jesus wasn't afraid to make himself vulnerable. Jesus, sitting on top of Jacob's well in John chapter 4, is important imagery of what it meant for God to be on earth.

In *Jesus Through Middle Eastern Eyes*, Kenneth Bailey writes on the woman at the well and says that this minor point in Scripture was always translated literally.[2] That Jesus was sitting *on* the well. He explains that wells had capstones, which were large stones that sat on top of them. They preserved the water. Bailey says that the capstone on Jacob's well in Samaria is still in place today. Capstones are thick stones with small holes where you can lower a bucket. Bailey points out that Jesus was, in fact, sitting on the well. A simple point that has profound implications for the woman who was about to walk up to it needing to draw water. Jesus would make himself unescapable. He had placed himself between her and the resource that would quench her vulnerability. Jesus was unavoidable.

Bailey points out that Middle Eastern village women avoided the heat of the day, though John says this is exactly when the woman came to the well. Typically, they would get water in the morning and just before sundown. They also would travel in groups. The jars that they'd need to fill were heavy. It would be difficult to do alone. And yet, in the story, the woman showed up with no one to help her. Probably signifying that she saw herself as an outcast from the community. She was *hera*, a widow. A woman bereft, lacking the resources of official social male support.

Middle Eastern wells don't have buckets like the wells we may think of in the West. People had to bring their own. Bailey says it is likely Jesus had a bucket and easily could have asked the disciples to leave it since he was going to the well while they were going to the city. But he didn't. He had gone to the well, strategically placing himself in need of whoever would show up. He would need their bucket. He would need their help. The God of the universe, the King with a heavenly throne, had allowed himself to be vulnerable enough to legitimately need the help of a Samaritan woman. A woman who was bereft. Bailey notes that this sends a powerful message about how Jesus viewed missional theology: with a value on mutuality in service. If this were not the case, Jesus would have brought his own bucket.

Bailey writes that Jesus also would have needed to keep about twenty feet of space between himself and the woman. It was the culturally appropriate distance. But the text says that Jesus didn't move. Rather, he asked her for a drink. One theory of communication is called *proxemics*. It is the study of space. Nonverbal messages can communicate more powerfully than verbal ones. The level of space we keep between ourselves and others is actually symbolic of how we view our relationship with that person. The greater the space distance, the greater the relational distance. This is why when you are in a fight with your romantic partner, you move to the other end of the couch. It feels safer to keep physical space when you feel internal distance. This is also why we engage in nervous chatter in elevators. We are pressed into a confined space with a person who is a stranger. We aren't sure if we are safe. We aren't sure if we are vulnerable.

And so we say things like, "Brrr. Cold today." What does that even mean?

It is our way of reducing the uncertainty of the close-space situation we are in. We want to see how the other person responds. Do they smile? Do they nod? Do they comment something back about the temperature? Their receptivity gives us meaning. Someone who isn't trained to notice these things may find phrases about weather or traffic to be a meaningless interaction. But it isn't. It's how we gauge our environment. If they smile, we feel more at ease. We can trust that, though a stranger is in closer space to us than we feel is normal, it must be okay. There is no threat to our physical safety. Of course, people who live in cities and are used to being crammed into small spaces with strangers probably don't have this internal dialogue anymore. It is a normal part of their culture. Culture always plays a role in how we receive and perceive interactions, especially as it relates to space. Everything about what Jesus did in John chapter 4 was breaking cultural barriers.

Bailey says that in his forty years living in the Middle East, he never crossed the social boundary line of gender. In biblical times, you did not talk to a woman in a desolate area where there were not witnesses. A chief justice of the Sanhedrin in the second century BCE wrote that "one shouldn't talk excessively with his own wife," because it would distract him from his study of the Torah.[3] We read stories of Jesus with women through our twenty-first-century bias, but for the Bible's original readers this controversial behavior would have been profound. I cannot overstate this enough: Always pay attention to when Jesus is reinforcing the cultural practices of his day and when he is reforming the cultural practices of his day. And for the record, you don't get crucified for reinforcing cultural practices; you get crucified for reforming them. When it comes to the treatment of women, Jesus was a reformer.

There was Jesus, placing himself in need of a female social outcast. In this moment, they were two strangers, held by the reality of their humanity. They were two bodies in a desert. Two people who were thirsty. And Jesus was sitting *on* the well, in need of a bucket.

Bailey notes that this is a posture that all Christians should continue to take. To serve but also to remain in a position that leaves you in need of service. Bailey argues that to serve from a position of power is not true service. We affirm people's dignity when we allow them to meet our needs as well. Vulnerability for the Christian is meant to be embraced, not avoided. To follow our calling is to wind up with our throats dry over and over again. This doesn't mean you are failing. It means you are succeeding at being human.

John 4 is Isaiah 41:17 in action: "The poor and the needy seek water, but there is none; their tongues are parched with thirst. I will answer them. I am the LORD, the God of Israel. I will not abandon them" (csb). Just like the woman would learn in John 4, we have access to a well that will never run dry. We have access to a King who is willing to leave his kingdom, to remake on earth what has been made in heaven, but he will need your help. I'd also like to note that we never do get the name of the woman at the well, but over and over, wherever the gospel is told, the world has been impacted by her story.

John 4:39 reads, "Now many Samaritans from that town believed in him because of what the woman said when she testified" (csb). The impact of our lives is often more important than our titles. We can choose to partake in the blessings of God despite our circumstances. The woman at the well would become a bucket in the hands of God, giving water to others who were thirsty.

There are going to be moments along this journey when you will need help more than you need your pride. And take note that when the Lord is leading, he will lead you into situations where he will allow you to need the service of others. This is a blessing, not a punishment. He himself had no bucket even though he reached the well. You won't have all the answers. That would rob you of seeking counsel. You won't have all the resources. That would rob you of mutuality of service. I believe on this journey of dreams and calling, life and passion, we will all find ourselves at one point or another as a body in a desert, with a capstone that looks too heavy to lift alone. So don't lift it alone. Humble yourself to receive the aid of your community. In doing so, you affirm their dignity.

All over the world today, those of us who feel bereft are working in isolation. We try not to share our inadequacies. We have snuck out at the hottest part of the day in hopes that no one will see us and that we won't have to point out our deficiency. But John reminds us of a God who is willing to journey with you into the desert. He is sitting *on* the well you need to draw from. He has made himself unavoidable. He is the access point to life. There is no way around the vulnerability that is going to be required of us.

In the story of my friend that I told in the beginning, I do want to share with you what happened. I want to encourage you if you are in a season of deficiency. Sometimes other people's carelessness can leave us feeling alone. But God always sees. The Lord did bring my friend a new job. And to be honest, it was better, in every metric, than the job she had lost. She survived her pilgrimage into the wilderness. It's one of the themes of Scripture. Water and desert. Streams and dry ground.

And a God throughout the journey who makes himself unavoidable.

> The person who trusts in the LORD,
>> whose confidence indeed is the LORD, is blessed.
>> He will be like a tree planted by water:
>> it sends its roots out toward a stream,
>> it doesn't fear when heat comes,
>> and its foliage remains green.
>> It will not worry in a year of drought
>> or cease producing fruit.
>
> Jeremiah 17:7–8 CSB

DIVE DEEPER

1. What does Heather mean by "mutuality of service"?
2. What does Bailey mean when he says that serving with power is not service?
3. If God is the well of living water that the earth needs, what does it mean when Heather says that we are "buckets"?

CHAPTER 12

THE GOLDEN SCEPTER

NO ONE'S COMING.

It hit me like a ton of bricks. I think I had spent most of my life thinking someone was coming to help me. Someone was going to open a door for me. Someone was going to tell me how to achieve what I was certain God was calling me into. Like Daedalus for Icarus, someone would craft my wings, and I would fly.

But I had no resources. No connections. No money. No team. And to be honest, very little vision. I didn't know how I was supposed to be faithful with my passion if God was going to provide me so few tools to work with. I was certain for many years that eventually someone would come. Like Elijah training Elisha, or the widow of Zarephath who was about to make her last meal and die, or the Samaritan woman talking to Jesus at the well, I needed some godly intervention.[1] I needed someone to come and help me. My well was running dry.

I had a conversation with my friend who happens to be a celebrity chef, Danielle Kartes. You may recognize her name from the *Kelly Clarkson Show* or *Good Morning America*, where she whips up delicious recipes and makes you laugh so hard your stomach hurts. Danielle had become a fast friend for me. We felt like we were at similar places in our careers and bonded over feeling like we wouldn't ever be good enough. We both also love food, which is a prerequisite for friendship in many female circles.

"It feels like I have been waiting for someone with a golden scepter," Danielle said while we were both commiserating about how hard it is to follow your giftings when passion leads to financial suffering.

"I had been waiting for someone to wave their golden scepter at me, and suddenly that's when everything would fall into place, and all of this wouldn't be so hard." She spoke with so much knowing, it felt like her brain had suctioned the words right from my frontal lobe.

"No one's coming," I said back to her. It was the first time I realized I meant it.

No one was going to come and help me do what I felt God had called me to. No one was going to give me a safety net in case I failed. It felt like no one was going to sponsor my visa to the promised land. If I wanted to do it, I would have to do it myself. In my situation, I wanted to be careful not to run ahead of God. I had been waiting on a sign from him that I was on the right path. That I wasn't crazy. I wanted confirmation that waiting on the Lord would renew my strength. But all I felt was depleted.

Have you ever designated in January what your word of the year will be? Well, one December I thought about what word truly defined the year I'd just had. What word best encapsulated my last twelve months of perceived failures. My dad's health was declining. I became obsessed with running the numbers of what his care would cost my family. My mom spends a lot of her energy supporting my grandma who is in her nineties and my dad who is terminally ill. I didn't know how to lighten her mental load; it just kept feeling like money would be the solution. With money we could afford to have someone be with my dad in her home every day, which is where he felt most comfortable. We wouldn't have to worry about what nursing home aid would cost. It makes you physically sick, by the way, calculating the cost of care for people who mean everything to you. If I just stopped with all this passion nonsense and focused on a corporate career rather than ministry, I could make more money. I could help ease my family's burdens. It felt like I was failing my parents.

All I could see were the years my dad had spent doing what he felt God had called him to and how it felt in these moments that the math wasn't mathing. It felt like God had abandoned him. Like God discards our buckets when they struggle to keep up with the water they hold. Because I knew how talented my father was, and also how much integrity he maintained with every step following his calling, I was growing more and more hurt, thinking what little he had to show for it. And when I say little, I mean what he accrued from it financially. I was deep in my earthly vision of things. My heart wanted to focus on heavenly impact, but my flesh was weak.

I was hurt. I was hurt because it felt like it would be so easy for God to have blessed my dad's efforts then, or my efforts now, and allow us not to worry. "God will take care of me," my dad always told us. He had never been worried. But worry was all I felt. For many years I was able to keep going because I had hope that something would change. That the golden scepter would appear. That God would send someone to tell me how to make money or monetize my passion better.

So much of my prayer life has felt like being alone on an island. No matter how many times I tried to swim out, call for help, build a raft, and attempt to paddle toward land, I would end up back where I started. Waiting for God to answer your prayer can be lonely. Other people can toss you coconuts, provide some shade, do things that ease the seclusion of the experience, but what you really need is to get off the island.

I've seen boats in the distance. I've seen the flash of a golden scepter. I have even had people tell me they'll be right back with an exit plan, but then nothing happens. They forget. But you remember. Eventually you end up in this space where you aren't even sure if it's worth it to keep screaming. Your throat hurts. Your arms are tired. It feels emotionally easier just to watch the boats sail by without hoping you can still get on one. You start to mumble out loud so your brain can audibly get the memo: "No one is coming."

I knew what Danielle was talking about. She was tired of feeling all alone on an island. She was tired of water and desert. She was tired of getting her hopes up. Hope, when you swear you are on your own, can have you feeling delusional. I know what it feels like to sit night after night huddled around a dying fire. I know what it feels like to want to ignore the possibility opening itself before you. I know what it feels like to want the right things for the right reasons, and be willing to do the work to get it, and yet none of your effort seems to matter.

What do we do when we see the flash of a golden scepter or hear the hum of a helicopter propeller but are too scared to let ourselves trust any of it because we have been here before? The truth is, though, if we were really on an island, we would yell even if our voices were hoarse. We would jump up and down and wave our arms. We wouldn't be afraid that we looked stupid, and we wouldn't wait to see how everything played out. We would be on our feet in anticipation. We would focus on the sound of the helicopter, even in the distance. The darkest I ever felt was when I started to believe that no one was coming. I started to doubt my own theology of a God who shows up beside wells in the desert. In that season of my life, the only word I could think of to describe what I was learning and unlearning about who God was, and what he was willing to do to reach me, was *stripped*.

So much of me was stripped that year. Things that I was certain were true no longer felt true. Dreams I had spent years cultivating no longer felt worth dreaming. Even my understanding of how God worked in suffering was suddenly no longer something I understood.

It felt as though so much of the meat and muscle that I thought God and I were building with each other in my body had been stripped clean off the bone.

I'd been stripped of what I thought made me who I was. And yet the hand-to-heart truth is that I was absolutely certain I was still in the presence of God. I was walking in my passions, I was suffering surely, but I also couldn't shake that God had called me into the desert. That he had placed me on the island. That I wasn't alone at all, even when it appeared that way.

It's how I learned one thing that I am now sure is the backbone of my new theology: Your circumstances don't determine God's presence. God's presence, despite your circumstances, is a wonder only the boniest of Christians can articulate. I don't know if I will ever take advice from Christians again if they can't describe for me the bones. If they can't point to where their imprint has been left in the sand from all their years of waiting. Show me how you continued to be still before the Lord, despite every taunting voice inside of you that shouted, "No one is coming." Show me your passion that's connected each bone. There are some lessons—not about God, but about ourselves, our hearts, and our motives—that I don't think we can learn until we sit on an empty island. Until helicopters that you thought were coming only kick the dust into your eyes and leave.

"Don't you care that I am in the wilderness?" we cry to a God we aren't sure is listening.

What do we do with years where we are doing the right things, serving in the right spaces, and following our passions and yet are still stripped before the Lord? A skeleton on an island. A body in the desert. A thirsty traveler beside a capstone that is too heavy for their arms and there is no Savior at the well.

From one bony Christian to another, please know that the Lord is near. His presence is the only reason we are still standing. You would have quit long ago if it wasn't for the Spirit of God allowing you to endure. And something tells me that what will be born from these dry bones will be more beautiful than we can even fathom. All I can think of is Ezekiel 37:5–10. Verses I have had marked for years in my Bible, long before I knew what it felt like to stand in the presence of the Lord, stripped of all I thought made me who I was.

> "This is what the Lord GOD says to these bones: I will cause breath to enter you, and you will live. I will put tendons on you, make flesh grow on you, and cover you with skin. I will put breath in you so that you come to life. Then you will know that I am the LORD."
>
> So I prophesied as I had been commanded. While I was prophesying, there was a noise, a rattling sound, and the bones came together, bone to bone. As I looked, tendons appeared on them, flesh grew, and skin covered them, but there was no breath in them. He said to me, "Prophesy to the breath, prophesy, son of man. Say to it: This is what the Lord GOD says: Breath, come from the four winds and breathe into these slain so that they may live!" So I prophesied as he commanded me; the breath entered them, and they came to life and stood on their feet, a vast army. (CSB)

The Creator is also the covenant keeper. The death and resurrection of Christ brought breath to all our bones. And there is often a similar pattern in our lives of death and resurrection. Dying to what we thought we were so we can be born into what God would have us become.

Something happens when you think God has stepped back from you. Eventually, you step forward toward him. This cycle is one of the most important elements of the Christian walk. Spiritual growth is not just about discovering who God is. It is also about discovering who we are in God. I couldn't answer that question honestly until I believed that no one was coming. The experience has marked me forever. When all is stripped away, I know who I really am.

The desert doesn't leave you, even long after you leave it.

"Look, I am about to do something new;
>   even now it is coming. Do you not see it?
>   Indeed, I will make a way in the wilderness,
>   rivers in the desert."

Isaiah 43:19 CSB

DIVE DEEPER

1. What does Heather mean by "bony Christian"?
2. When did you feel like you were on an island alone, waiting on a miracle from God?
3. Is there a way you can show up for someone else who may be feeling like no one is coming?

CHAPTER 13

WHY ARE YOU HERE?

I WAS SITTING IN MY CAR, PARKED IN MY DRIVE-way. There was no place I needed to go, and the engine wasn't even running. But there I was, sitting behind the wheel, ten feet outside of my house. No one was home, but I was nervous the walls would hear me.

"Why are you here?" my mentor, José, asked me over the phone. He didn't mean in my car, he meant on the planet. "Why are you here?" His deep voice radiated over the speaker.

It had been eleven months since I'd last talked to him. I knew exactly how long it had been because, as I wrote earlier, I count. I post-stamp everything. I have a prayer journal where I keep all the dates. I track the hand of God over my life like an air traffic controller. I know the last prayer he answered, and I know how long I prayed in between. I view my spiritual life like a treasure map, and I am always putting in new pegs so I can see big themes along the journey. If you are cool with being a religious fanatic, I highly recommend this spiritual practice. It has changed the way

I pray. It has changed the way I experience God. I don't question whether God is real, because I have pages and pages of notes of God's involvement in my life. I've never doubted whether the divine works in and through humanity. I have a diary of his every movement.

Keeping a track record of my spiritual life is how my faith has grown feet. I told God a long time ago that I didn't think I was capable of faith that could move mountains. I didn't even have a step stool. I prayed probably about six years ago now for God to build my faith. I don't see faith as something I give God as much as it is something God builds within me, something that I can now stand on. Faith is built through experiences where God has been found trustworthy. I can't conjure up experiences I haven't had, but I can pray for eyes to see and ears to hear all that God is trying to work out in my life. Prayer is not solely our telling God what we see. It should also involve our submitting ourselves before the Lord so that God can reveal in us what God sees.

"If you build it, I will stand on it," I told him. I didn't know back then what I know now. That God loves to build.

My prayer journal is not simply a place to write down my thoughts, though I do that from time to time. It is how and where I map out all my spiritual coordinates. I am telling you this in case you are looking for a way to tangibly experience your spiritual life. Every time I have a big prayer, I write it in my prayer journal with the date above the request. Two years ago, I added another piece to my visual need of faith scaffolding. I started building an altar.

If a prayer in my prayer journal gets answered, I take a rock (you can order small ones on Amazon) and, with a paint marker, write a keyword to connect the prayer I had prayed on the rock with the date I first prayed it and then the date it was answered. I then place the rock into a basket. That basket sits by my fireplace. I see it regularly. So does everyone who comes inside.

I have told God, "One day, that basket will overflow, and I will have built you an altar." But really it is God who built it. I'm simply a recordkeeper. I have eyes to see and ears to hear what God is already doing. Last week, I added another rock to my basket. Another pillar to stand on. Another gift of God to build my faith. God loves to build.

Tracking God has helped me realize that you don't have to be a religious guru who has the sheer willpower to believe what you have not seen. God will give you a rock. God will give you experiences, but you have to have eyes to see it. All you have to do is keep record. I actually think God likes doing this. I think he has been waiting for someone to notice. To connect all the dots. To mark the movements. I truly believe God delights in our delighting in God.

Then one day when someone enters your home and tells you how discouraged they are and how little faith they have, you can pull out your basket of rocks. You can read them the dates that span years in between. You can let them hold, touch, and feel the physical symbol of all the gifts God has given you. All the faith he has allowed you to stand on. You can build God an altar. But really it is God who builds it. Because God loves to build.

I often write down the dates of when I talk to José as well, with notations on the conversation. He is filled with spiritual wisdom, and there is seldom a day we speak that he doesn't say something worth writing down. I love learning from people like that. People who have so much God inside of them that it spills over onto everyone around them. José reminded me of my father. Another man who had spent a great deal of time alone in his prayer room. A man who had built his house on rocks of faith. It's why I struggled talking to José anymore.

When my mom came home from work one day last October, she found my dad unresponsive. She called me in a panic, and Seth and I drove straight to her. I watched my husband, the man I love the most in this world, pick up the limp body of my father, the man I adore the most in this world, and carry him to the backseat of my mother's car. She drove him straight to the ER. He had suffered a massive seizure and would spend twenty-four hours on a ventilator. After we found my dad, do you know what I did? I went to teach my class. And my sister finished her reports for her patients. We knew we had to because we didn't know what would happen next or if we would be gone from work for an indefinite period of time. As I boxed up my emotions and taught my students, I knew they had no idea what was going on in my life. Rarely do any of us have any clue what is going on in other people's lives. Every day, we small-talk our way right past people who are immensely suffering.

"What's going on with the weather?" we awkwardly exchange to one another while shuffling back to our own office. It's the adult rite of passage. The theory of proxemics.

The songwriter of Disney's *Frozen* nailed it in these lyrics: "Don't let them in, don't let them see, be the good girl, you always have to be, conceal, don't feel, put on a show, make one wrong move, and everyone will know."[1] Every church I speak in, I remind myself of this. Despite smiling faces, I remind myself that these are people and that people are suffering. I assume I am getting up to say something to someone who is just like me. Someone who is secretly falling apart. It informs the messages I write.

After seeing my dad, my prayer warrior, my man of faith and altar builder, lying on a hospital bed with the hum of a machine that was keeping him breathing, I struggled to know what to do with all my faith. I didn't know how to place this moment in a basket of rocks. Sometimes faith feels cruel. It smells of delusion.

His Alzheimer's got so much worse after that seizure, which would just be the beginning of more seizures to come. On my daughter's twelfth birthday, my mom, sister, and I walked him to lie down in the back room away from the party. His brain gets overstimulated if he is around too many people. There were decorations in the living room. A cake on the counter uncut. But in the back room, my dad stopped breathing twice before the anti-seizure medication kicked in. I crawled up onto the bed with him and held his hand. My brother at his feet, my sister on the other side, and my mom hovering above him.

"You were such a good dad to me," I whispered into his ear. I told him this because he was.

Our food was cold by the time we came back to the main area of the house, still full of laughing people.

Conceal, don't feel, put on a show . . .

Once Dad was able to stand again, we all sang happy birthday to my daughter, London. The nice thing about Alzheimer's is that you can have a massive seizure at your granddaughter's birthday party one moment and happily eat cake an hour later. You don't remember any of it. But I do. And so do my siblings. My mom carries these pieces of her everywhere she goes. That parallel image of the husband she used to have side by side with the reality of who he has become. Happy memories now darkened by sadness and suffering.

Make one wrong move, and everyone will know.

All around us, people are suffering. It's the adult rite of passage.

I did a prayer walk with my dad a few days after he was released from the hospital. I walked the block with him and my mom and prayed with tears rolling down my face.

"Please heal my dad," I said out loud.

I didn't usually speak like this in front of him. It feels irresponsible to acknowledge the elephant while it's in the room with you. But I couldn't help myself. I am not above begging.

"Please, Lord, restore him to us for some period of time."

I know it isn't likely. I have faith, not delusion. But I've continued to ask God to heal him anyway. I will do it until he's gone. I'd love my dad to see what I am doing in ministry. I'd love him to hear me preach a sermon. He would be so proud to see his legacy continued. To see that his prayers did not expire. Sometimes I think my dad would like me more as an adult. I've grown so much since he knew me last. I bet we would have a lot in common.

After a few seconds of no one else talking on our prayer walk, my dad said, "Lord, I think there was something you wanted me to do, but I would need your help to still do it. Will you help me?"

The date was October 28, 2023. I know because I wrote it down. My mom and I looked at each other, stunned. It had been a long time since I had heard my dad acknowledge his former life or his incessant "I'm going to pour out" in ministry phrases. We had just gotten him off a ventilator. He was struggling to know our names. There was a delusional piece of me that started to believe he could come back from this. Maybe this was only the beginning. Maybe God would restore him to us for even a few months. Maybe my dad would be able to know me as an adult. Maybe I could read him this page. Maybe we would go to the prayer room together and praise God for what he had done.

Within the coming weeks of that prayer, his memory only declined. He struggles now to finish sentences. He points a lot and stops speaking midthought. That prayer, on October 28 (a few days shy of another November), is the last prayer I have heard my dad pray aloud. And all he said, his dying wish, was to finish what he believed he and God had started. These are his passion pains. And no neurological disorder, disease, or seizures could make him forget.

"I've been very depressed," I told José that day from my car. If he could see me having this conversation from my driveway in a car that wasn't even on, he probably would have gathered as much. I was struggling to keep teaching, writing, and making dinner. I was grieving my daddy. I didn't know how to talk to José anymore, a man who reminded me so much of my father. I didn't know how to have conversations about faith and the plans and promises of God. I didn't know how to track a God who had brought me into deep water when it felt like I would drown. I was just trying to make it through the day.

"Why are you here?" he asked me again. He didn't mean in my driveway. He meant on this earth. "Why are you here? Once you can answer that question, all the other questions fall into place. Pray for the Lord to reveal this to you."

After we hung up, I sat in silence for a few moments in the stillness of my car. My doubt and frustration and disappointment hung in the air like a fog. That night I woke up at 12:06 a.m. I know because I wrote it down.

"I am here to help people who are depleted, doubting, and discouraged from giving up hope," I typed into the notes app on my phone. "My goal is to encourage one person to take one more step, one more time, for one more day." I thought of my dad mustering the brainpower to pray one last time.

That's what I knew most intimately. How to track the hand of God one more time and let it get you through the day. I knew how to take the hand of my dying father and lead him on one more prayer walk. I got a tattoo on my right wrist so that I'd never forget why I am here. It says one word, a word that reminds me on dark days of my passion, my calling, and my purpose. In black ink, on brown skin, the word *endure* is written in cursive letters. It looks much more elegant and delicate than living it has felt.

I stare at it often. When I am doubting, depleted, and discouraged. *Endure*, my wrist speaks back to me.

"One more step, one more time, for one more day."

I wrote it on a rock and placed it on my altar.

Let us not get tired of doing good, for we will reap at the proper time if we don't give up.

Galatians 6:9 CSB

DIVE DEEPER

1. What are you grieving that has made "great big faith" feel heavier?
2. Do you have a prayer journal? Does it help encourage you? And if you don't have one, would you be interested in getting one? Why or why not?
3. Why are you here?

CHAPTER 14

DO YOU TRUST ME?

"CAN I ASK YOU A QUESTION?" MY THERAPIST ASKED.

"Are you able to separate you, and I mean your personhood, from this project? Is it possible that not hitting goals in the project doesn't at all connect to your personhood?"

I realize I was paying this woman to sober me of my self-wallowing, but I wasn't ready for such a fast-absorbing tonic. It was like for the first time my brain was considering whether I was a separate person from the work I was trying to produce. I kid you not, it had never occurred to me to think of myself as being separate from my creative labor. When we are in our passions so deeply, it often is hard to decipher where we end and the project begins. We had felt like cojoining limbs. And I thought that was a sign of my devotion, not a sign of my emotional deficiency. I had spent so much time feeling bewildered at God for failing me. But what if God hadn't failed "me"? What if only the project failed? What if I was separate from the things I was producing?

Have you ever followed God in creating something only to feel failed by him when that thing fails? I know it's possible because I've experienced it. I really need you to sit with me in this for a second, considering that we and whatever we produce may not be a singular entity. What if your dream is not who you are? What if this business or law school or med school or career or book or ministry or relationship is a separate thing from *you*? What if *you* will still be *you* without it? Who you actually are is more creative and resilient than any singular outlet. What if failing in that one area doesn't mean you're a failure? When a project fails, can it be sad, heartbreaking, and painful but also separate from your personhood? Eventually we need to define for ourselves who we actually are. Why are you here?

I never set out to have a podcast. It was something I had discussed doing with another person at one point but then didn't feel it was the right time. I wrote the title in my notes app on my phone. I prayed, *Lord, if you want me to do this, send me the resources to do it in the right season.* And then I just kind of moved on. I don't like doing things I am not absolutely certain God called me to. It feels far too risky. Too much deep water. My legs are tired of treading. A full year after I had prayed this prayer, Ed Gilbreath, who would become my executive producer for my podcast, *Viral Jesus*, contacted me.

"If you had the support of my organization and our resources, what would you create?" he asked me. I opened up the notes app on my phone, and I read him the title of the podcast I had thought about doing a year before but then decided against. Within a few months, Ed and I were off to the races. We were podcasters now. And I was certain that this was going to work because I had not run ahead of God. I had waited on him. I had waited till he sent for me. And God had stirred a little golden scepter to twirl around me and make things materialize. And you want to know what happened? Year one, the show was off to a nice start. Year two, we were gaining momentum. Year three, we were seeing answered prayers and breakthrough. I even have a prayer rock in my basket confirming as much. But by year four, nothing was moving. Downloads stopped growing but the work required of me didn't. I was pouring countless hours into producing a show that wasn't expanding. What was especially disorienting for me was that I knew God had called me to do it.

What do we do when God doesn't operate by the guidelines we thought he operated by? Sometimes you are patient and faithful and wait for the right signs so you know you can be absolutely certain God is going before you, only to have him seemingly stop blessing your effort. And it can feel confusing. What happens when God gets you through the valley but then stops you just before the summit of the mountain? It can feel like whiplash when we trust that God led us to apply to the program but now we sense God telling us to leave it. I am never quite sure how to hold my faith when I am letting so much else go. What is the obligatory Christian response for when we come up just a bit short? The truth I have learned through experience is that sometimes God calls us to things for a season. And just like seasons eventually change, so will your calling. And I am learning that it doesn't mean you failed; it means you fulfilled the season. It accomplished its work in you. It is okay to move into the next season.

Trusting in God isn't some mysterious thing I will into existence. My trust in him would probably be more impressive if it was. Remember, I don't see faith as something I have built but rather as something God has gifted to me, little by little, step by step, stone by stone. The task for me then comes in trying to honor all that God has built in my past as steady ground for me to stand on in my present. Faith can be complicated. It is a word that can have a lot of baggage attached to it.

Sometimes it feels like having faith means I believe in a plan or a purpose or a soon-coming deliverance from whatever trial I am in. When people tell me, "You have to have faith," I feel like they are telling me I have to have the right beliefs attached to my circumstances for God to see me as good or worthy. The reality is that some days I don't know what I think, much less what I believe. God has been very good about not letting me feel like I have the divine all figured out.

I have spent a lot of energy in my life trying to force myself to believe whatever I thought would be the appropriate Christian belief for the situation I was navigating. *How would a faithful Christian respond to this scenario?*

All this works out fine until life strips you of everything you thought you believed. Until you find yourself in a moment that doesn't match the way you thought God was obligated to respond. There are some circumstances that no one gives you a Christian script for. Some failures you never saw coming. And the idea that God not only saw them but didn't warn you, or worse, directed you toward it, can feel like enough to make the ground shift beneath your feet.

In *The Sin of Certainty* by biblical scholar Peter Enns, you get a vocabulary shift for all the baggage wrapped up in your faith understanding.[1] The premise of his book is that while the Greek word for "faith," *pistis*, does describe beliefs, there is a complementary component to it that people often overlook. *Pistis* has an underlying property of trust. Enns argues that we must be careful not to trust our beliefs about God more than God himself. The gospel ultimately is not about right thinking or beliefs. The gospel is not about our own moral superiority. The gospel is not about us at all. It is about who Jesus is and what he did within the context of the Jewish story that now brings living water to all the world. He brought order out of chaos. God is committed to humanity, despite humanity.

The reason this shift is so important is because there may be days when you don't know what you believe anymore, and when that happens it becomes much more important that you know who you trust. Faith is about our trusting in the work that Jesus did. Essentially Enns believes that faith is not a "what" but a "who."

"Do you trust me?" God is asking us in every single circumstance that has stripped us of everything we thought we knew. "Do you trust me enough to start something? Do you trust me enough to end it? Do you trust me on the mountain? Do you trust me in the desert? Do you trust me enough to fall? Do you trust me enough to fly? Do you trust me in the shallows? Do you trust me in the deep? Do you trust me with your money? Do you trust me with a negative balance?" Trust is the currency by which faith is always transacted. And just when you think you have a handle on how to trust in God, the ground shifts beneath you and you have to ask yourself whether you trust him in this new, unfamiliar terrain. Your life is what prepares you for your life. Living it fully present and embodied within the highs and lows is how we learn and experience faith.

For some reason, this idea that faith doesn't require me to force a belief but instead to cling to whom I trust has removed so much weight from me. I can tell you in all honesty that I do trust God. I know this because I know who I am when the chaos waters rise. I don't always understand God. I don't know how heavenly rules of engagement operate. I don't know why there is so much suffering or what plan God is working out in my life. But I do know I can trust God without knowing much of anything else. I do believe that trust is the actual story, not the wins and losses. Our ability to receive a God we could never earn is a beautify testimony.

It's not that I don't have faith (right beliefs) in God; it's that for much of my life I have struggled to have faith in God's plans for me. The word *faith* often feels complex when I am staring at my own inadequacies. *Can God still do something with me? With this? Did he change his mind about me?* Are we supposed to be able to muster up a bunch of right words and right beliefs in order to convince him we will be worth the effort? Is God watching to see if we flinch? Will he burn our wings if we get too close to the sun on this? Is it enough if 70 percent of our imagination still feels like passion is worth having? What's the over-under on what God needs in a "faithful vessel"?

I think of Abraham, who "believed the LORD, and he credited it to him as righteousness" (Genesis 15:6).

But it isn't just that Abraham believed God existed. He believed in his promises over his life. Abraham waited twenty-five years to hold the son God promised he would have. I have no doubt those twenty-five years felt like fifty. It's not lost on me that Abraham believed in God's promise. Not just a promise for him but a promise that would come to pass *through* him. Abraham believed that his passion was worth suffering through. That God was putting a broader story together that would far exceed the story of his one life.

And yet, even with a spiritual patriarch like Abraham, there are places where his right beliefs didn't match his actions. For example, he slept with his bondwoman in an attempt to bring the promise of a son into fruition through Hagar, his slave, rather than Sarah, his wife. I never liked how that story ended. Hagar got used for her body and her womb and then was suddenly sent away, and it all just feels like trauma.

It is fascinating how biblical stories will give you this type of character complexity. This is why I told you earlier the Bible is not about us or people like Abraham; it is about how the people of Israel saw God and God's commitment to the people of Israel despite Israel. God remains committed to humanity despite humanity. The Bible is always pointing you to Jesus. Jesus fulfills what complex human biblical characters could not. The Creator is the Covenant Keeper. It is often hard to know when reading the Bible who is good and who is bad. Because that person is never the point of the story. Seeing God work in and through biblical characters, through the Jewish story and culminating in the cross, is the point. We have been redeemed. Jesus is always the point. That's who we are supposed to be tracking. Is Solomon good or bad? Is David good or bad? Is Naomi good or bad? Is Sarah good or bad? If you are able to answer that question too quickly, I would insist you've not looked closely enough at the stories. God causes the sun to shine on both the righteous and the wicked.

We often focus on the faith of Abraham, but what about the faith of Hagar? Did she always have the right beliefs even while wandering a desert? How true did the promise of God feel over her life, and her son, while she was placing his body by a bush so she didn't have to watch him die (Genesis 21:15–16)? Was she 30 percent sure God would show up and do something? Ten percent? How much "faith" was God working with in that desert? What amount of "right belief" did Hagar give to get God's attention? I hope you can see now that the gospel is not about what you give God but about what God has given you. My friend David Asscherick told me once, "God isn't demanding your righteousness. God is providing you righteousness." Jesus is the point.

Genesis 21:16 ends with Hagar crying, and verse 17 begins with God's response. There is something really beautiful about that to me. There is no sermon. There is no monologue. There is not even a prayer where Hagar tells God all the things she still believes he can do. There is no monument. There is no offering. There is no song or revival. There is a striking lack of detail. And maybe that is intentional. Verse 16 literally ends by saying, "And as she sat there, she began to sob." Finally, some character development I can relate to.

Scripture says that she cried, and God heard. That's it. That was the exchange. This was what the biblical writer found to be the most relevant detail. Faith was not a *what* for Hagar. Faith became a *who*. Hagar didn't earn redemption; God just gave it. God didn't demand her righteousness; God provided her righteousness. The story reveals to us who God is despite who we are. What does faith in this story look like? Does it look like something Hagar gave God or something God gave her? Hagar has had an experience with God. God has proven himself to be trustworthy. And the Hebrews wrote it down. The story would be passed from generation to generation so that everyone remembered that they were a part of a larger story. They tracked the movement of God in the story of them as a people.

In every situation and circumstance, God is asking, "Do you still trust me?" That is the human experience. And to be honest, I understand if there are moments when it feels like you don't know anymore if you can. I don't think God's posture toward you is dependent that much on your being "good" in every situation. I am discovering that God is capable of being good with or without us. God is committed to you. You won't earn his favor. And it doesn't seem fair when we are so used to earning things.

I have had students sit in my office and say, "I've never felt so far from God." And I always find this ironic. "People who are far from God," I tell them, "rarely make appointments with their teacher to tell them they feel far from God." God is always closer than we think.

"Do you still trust me," God is asking, "even when I feel far?"

Earlier I told you about my friend who had started a business that looked like it was failing. We had sat across from each other eating chips and salsa, and she said, "I don't even know what I am doing. I don't even know if the business is going to work."

This week Cortney sold that business for a profit. She successfully built something that now will outlast her season within it. Her story now becomes part of a much larger one. Her yes has intersected with someone else's. And now, as I tell you the story, it broadens even more. Our lives and decisions always outlive us. This is why you must never think that your story doesn't matter. As we ate chips and salsa that day, she thought she might have been drowning. It turns out, however, that she was learning how to swim.

Trust in the LORD with all your heart and lean not on your own understanding.

Proverbs 3:5

DIVE DEEPER

1. Does the word *faith* bring up any baggage for you?
2. How do you know you can trust God in the situation you are in right now?
3. In what ways has God displayed himself as trustworthy in the past?

CHAPTER 15

FOOTPRINTS IN THE SNOW

I HAVE AN ONLINE FRIEND NAMED JAMIE. I SAY *online* because that is how we met, though our friendship has morphed into the real world. We got to know each other on social media. We prayed together, sent memes, rallied in the comments section around photos that warranted the validation of a complete stranger.

One day she was visiting family who lived near me. I suddenly understood why we had connected so quickly. The Midwestern cornfields had raised us both. Our childhoods in desolate environments brought out familiar traits in each of us. We met up for lunch. Then a year later I was speaking in DC, and we met up for dinner in her neck of the woods. Online friendship is one of the blessings of an otherwise complicated relationship that I have with technology. It can close so many miles of distance.

Jamie sent me a message after praying for the passion pains I had told her I was experiencing.

"I feel like you are wintering," she said.

"What is wintering?" I asked.

"It's a book by Katherine May.[1] Almost a metaphor for depression and darkness that comes like a wave in certain seasons. While we all would like a perpetual summer, the sun always gives way to winter."

I have, at various moments in my life, found myself in the longest of winters. None have felt quite as severe as the most recent. Michiganders learn quickly how to survive the snow. We've navigated a polar vortex or two. Maybe she was right. Maybe I was wintering. Maybe you are too.

Maybe the cold is uncomfortable, perhaps even unbearable. Maybe your hands and heart are covered in frost. Maybe your cheeks and toes are numb. I've knelt on knees I couldn't feel. It's hard for me to go outside when I am wintering. It's easier, and sometimes necessary, to bundle up and start a fire. A fireplace is a nonnegotiable for Seth and me. It's how you trick your mind into nostalgia for winter. We get to stock up on wood and hunker down until the blizzard passes. No one is demanding you pretend that life is something that it isn't. You just accept winter for what it is. And you realize that the only way out is through.

Once Jamie gave me that "wintering" vocabulary, it thawed something inside me that I had otherwise been resisting. By now you know how I feel about my prayer walks, times when I activate my body and my brain and pour my heart out to God while forcing my feet to hit the pavement. I went on a prayer walk one morning during this wintering period. I forced myself out of the house before the sun came up and, with hood over my head and my body shivering, I pressed through the cold. As I was walking, boots and thick socks wrapped around my feet like casts, I realized I had never done this in my prayer life before. Like any sane Michigander, I typically stopped my prayer walks by the end of November. Any prayers would have to be prayed indoors. But here I was, still walking through the sludge. A persistence was taking shape in me that only harsh elements could reveal.

I wasn't just passionate about books or ministry or a career.

I was passionate about God. A life deeply interconnected with the Lord was what I most sincerely wanted.

I was willing to track him through the storm. It would take more than cold hands to dissuade my need to see his presence guiding me.

"When stripped of everything else," I said out loud in air so unsympathetic I could see my breath, "you are all that remains in me."

I watched my boots make deep prints in the snow. I could hear them crunching ice beneath my feet. And that's when it dawned on me that there was a beauty in winter I could only have experienced with the level of desperation these harsh days had driven me to press into. When we think God has stepped back, sometimes we step forward. I had never been more desperate to see God guide me, and never more convicted that I'd find him even in all the snow. I had learned how to keep my feet moving forward, even in the winter. I had endured. And all around my block were the footprints of my faith. Or my trust. Whichever word feels like less baggage.

I had thought trials were meant to teach me about God. But in the winter I was starting to learn things about myself. When stripped of everything I thought I needed to be successful, I started seeing what was beneath all that fat. I could see the bones. We go into the cold hoping to see God, and in the harshest of winters, in the space most designed to reveal our steps, we are able to see ourselves.

Every footprint I saw as I paced my block in prayer somehow gave me a sense of the type of person I was becoming. The type of person we all become when passion leads us past our own suffering and into our purpose. I didn't know what would come or if this season would ever relent, but I did know one thing now that I couldn't have known until I saw those prints: I had been here before.

What do we do with the silence of God? What do we do with winters? What do we do when the last word we heard directly contradicts what we now see? What do we do when comfort feels like a false memory? When hope feels like delusion? We search the ground for footprints. And if we are lucky, we realize we have been here before. I don't know if that insight awakens something in you like it did for me. But I distinctly remember feeling comforted by it. Seeing who I was in the snow reminded me of where I'd been. Not only have we survived these elements before, but the hope is that we have developed tools within ourselves to navigate it better and better each time around. Because suffering will always be back. Laughter will always give way to silence. Seasons will always change. Nature has been telling us this all along.

Between the Old Testament prophecy and the New Testament fulfillment are four hundred years of silence. Between the Old Testament promises and their actualization are four hundred years of quiet. Between Malachi and Matthew sit four hundred years of confusion, wonder, hope, and stillness. We don't have to fear in days of silent wandering. We have been here before.

Speaking about a future prophet, long past Elijah's time, Malachi 4:5 reads, "See, I will send the prophet Elijah to you."

And then in Matthew 3, we meet the cousin of Jesus, John the Baptist, who would serve as the fulfillment to what we just read about "Elijah" in Malachi 4:5.

But in the space of that four hundred years, so much would have happened. There would have been comfort that felt like a false memory and hope that felt like delusion. And yet every Christmas, every winter, we remember the birth of Jesus. The King who would go to the cross and usher in the upside-down kingdom of heaven. A kingdom where the first shall be last and the last shall be first. A kingdom that would provide righteousness rather than demand it. Jesus would be the answer to all the prayers that felt unheard, unseen, or forgotten for more than four hundred years.

What do we do with the silence of God? What do we do when the last word we heard is in direct contradiction to what we now see? We remember that we have been here before. We look for our footprints, and if we are lucky, we can reveal them to someone else who has found themselves in the same cold. That's the thing about footprints. The goal is to leave some worth following.

"This won't last," we whisper to others stumbling their way through the snow. "Winter never does."

There are different seasons in life. And while I would love a perpetual summer, the earth will always give way to winter. What if instead of hunkering down and boarding your doors, you learned how to walk in the cold? What if you learned how to take a deep breath of icy air and let it remind you that you're alive? What if you looked at how the snow lies and let yourself acknowledge that even in this are specks of beauty? What if you simply let winter be a part of your season? It will not last. Seasons never do. So you may as well lean in and see what it has to teach you. See what this cold can reveal about who you are. Scan the snow for footprints. Trust the guide to lead you, just like all the times before. God is always closer than you think.

Underneath all that snow, the seeds and gardens are buried. The beauty isn't gone; sometimes it just gets buried. It's on pause. It's sleeping. Nature, like all things, needs rest. In fact, sometimes the harsher the winter, the livelier the spring. The thing about snow is that it eventually melts and saturates the ground. There are flowers that couldn't bloom if they hadn't gone through winter. There are species that thaw, and their hearts just keep on beating. There are diseases that can't be killed unless you freeze the ground they are hiding in.

So, what if you aren't failing? Or drowning? Or losing?

What if you are wintering? And seasons always change.

"The windstorm comes from its chamber, and the cold from the driving north winds. Ice is formed by the breath of God, and watery expanses are frozen."

Job 37:9–10 CSB

DIVE DEEPER

1. When have you "wintered" in your life?
2. What footprints can you look at in your life right now? How have you been here before?
3. Where in your past have you experienced what you thought was God's silence? How do you see that experience now?

CHAPTER 16

GOD DOESN'T NEED ME

I HAVE NEVER, AT ANY POINT IN MY LIFE, KNOWN financial abundance. Sometimes I'll compare myself to other people serving in similar giftings who do have financial blessings, and I feel like I'll never measure up.

I was not kidding when I told you I had dreamed of being rich and righteous. I've read Matthew 19:24 where Jesus said out loud, "Again I tell you, it is easier for a camel to go through the eye of a needle than for someone who is rich to enter the kingdom of God." And I've still been willing to take my chances.

Money doesn't motivate me, which is probably why I often have so little of it, but I do have financial burdens that take up a sweet minute of my daily prayer life. I know what it feels like to be sick just because you went to the grocery store. I know what it feels like to give to someone else out of what you sincerely don't have. I also know what it feels like to have someone reach out for help and not be able to support them. And not because you don't want to. But because if you do, you'll be short on your own payments. Most of us aren't trying to make money off our passions because we are greedy. We are just trying to figure out how to pay the water bill. We have only so much energy or hours in a day. Nursing home care for aging parents or spouses with disabilities that require external medical support can cost between $5,000 and $10,000 a month. Millions of Americans feel like they are drowning.

I make a decent living from my teaching salary, but I'm a millennial with a PhD. I have enough student loan debt to have purchased a second home, but without the second home. I have three kids whom we often keep in private education, and a dad who at some point in the not-so-distant future will need full-time care. All this weighs on me. If I die young, educational loan debt will be why. My life costs more money than my Christian school salary could ever provide me. I am lucky that I have a husband who is skilled in the trades. He has always been able to do side hustles on top of his full-time job in order to pay the kids' school bill. I know that I am still far more financially blessed and stable than many other people. Still, on most days we are one water heater or furnace breakdown away from financial ruin. Sometimes our passions cost us more than we ever receive from them.

I will tell you that the past couple of years of my life have probably been my best financially. If you read *It's Not Your Turn*, you know that I have had my card declined when purchasing paper plates. Nothing springs me into action quicker than seeing someone whose card just got declined. I have an internal homing beacon that draws me to lines where people may have insufficient funds. Without a second thought I will put your groceries on my credit card if it spares you even a moment of the secondhand embarrassment I have known so deeply. I have been there, and once you walk through that fire, you have a nose with a special detector for smoke. So, while opening your bank account app and seeing single digits is enough to make you panic before inserting your card at the gas station, I will say that my late thirties have been far better to me than my twenties or early thirties. Now if we could just do something about the cost of living.

Because I was so poor as a young mom when Seth and I were both in school, I now am always grateful just not to be negative. Hallelujah and praise the Lord. I have credit cards that aren't even close to being maxed out, and I will tell you that at twenty-nine I did not have this testimony (hang in there, Gen Z, it gets better). But because I am not by any means wealthy, I still feel the weight of all my financial burdens. And your passion, in its very nature of suffering, takes energy. Energy you could be spending on a more economically wise endeavor.

"I don't know if I would still be doing this if it wasn't for my dad," I said to the Lord while on a prayer walk the other day. He started his ministry in the 1980s and always believed that the Lord would finish it. I can still see him totally defeated, sitting by his computer after reading an email that a television pilot he had just spent the entire summer filming wasn't going to get the budget of the investors to move forward. It was the last project he would work on before the Alzheimer's diagnosis. It broke his heart, and then I'm convinced that his heart broke his body. His show was good, really good, and yet God didn't bless it. It's how I am able to tell you right now that what you are doing may be beautiful, wonderful, cutting-edge work and yet still not draw an increase. It doesn't mean you are doing anything wrong; it doesn't mean you are not called, and it doesn't mean this is not your gift. Passion is not about what we do because it's flourishing. It's about what we can't help but do despite the suffering. My father taught me that.

I've kept notes and media files of that television show for years. I have the promo DVD in my glove box, though no one uses DVDs anymore. I couldn't play it if I wanted to. I even turned his concept into a book pitch I sent off seven years ago to a publisher, which was turned down. Another passion project to add to my rejection pile. I've wanted to finish his work. I've felt compelled to finish his work. I've felt spiritually responsible to finish his work. And yet ministries and religious television programming and products cost money. And while I have been rich in love, money has never been something I've had in abundance. But, like I said, I have been here before.

I spoke at a Christian conference one fall. It was one of those big ones led by a celebrity. They pack stadiums and there is incredible music, and you'd have to be Lucifer himself not to be moved by the Spirit when surrounded by that many people pleading for God to show up in their lives. I got back to my hotel room close to midnight and sat in the shower and cried. I had just been in a room with so many people pursuing their passions for ministry in a national way. At this one conference, in less than ten minutes, they raised over $100,000 toward ministry aid. It floored me. I would never be able to do what these leaders were able to do for God. I would never be able to have that same impact.

"God doesn't need me," I said loud enough for my own ears to get warm under the words.

And here is the thing. Sometimes it helps, when you feel inferior beside someone else's greatness, to pick apart where they may be flawed. But I couldn't. They were all truly rich and righteous. They were so sincere and so gifted and so kind. A singer, whose name you would recognize if I wrote it here, squeezed my shoulder in the greenroom when I told a joke. She was so down to earth. She was the type of person who laughs at your punch line as if she had been your friend since middle school even though you just met her five minutes ago. She was ten times more lovely than I thought a person capable of being. There was nothing to pick apart. They all deserved every bit of the blessings they were reaping, and the kingdom of God was better for them having been there.

I had spoken at many conferences before. I had been in other crowds. But something about the warmth of this one made me feel emotional. I wasn't crying because I was so moved by God; I was crying because I realized for the first time that God didn't *need* me. God had lots of talented and godly people. I think somewhere in my mind I had thought that God would one day bless me because he needed me. Have you ever felt like that? Like you know that the motives of your own heart are pure, so you think maybe God needs people like you? He needed people with integrity whom he could trust. He needed good hearts who would be obedient to him. He needed thought leaders or medical professionals or sports players or lawyers or businesspeople or content creators or writers who weren't in it for money but were in it truly because of passion. But then I sat in a greenroom with dozens of leaders who were all those things and more. And I cried because I realized for the first time that God didn't actually need me to do what he was already very much doing pretty well without me. I get that this is actually a good thing, and I was happy for God, but I was also becoming disillusioned with myself. Where do you fit on a team that's already stacked?

Especially if you are a millennial like me, you go through the first half of your life with all these people telling you you're special, and at some point, you kind of hope it's true. And in the Christian world we can really let those ideas inflate us.

"For I know the plans I have for you," we tell each other, forgetting that Jeremiah 29:11 was written to an Israel that was in Babylonian exile. We love to take the Bible out of context if it will give us the confidence to buy a beach house. We are told every weekend at church that God has a purpose for our lives, and that purpose grows more grandiose by the day.

We often share these Bible verses to encourage one another when we experience life's chaos. But I discovered while putting together a Bible study series on the Good Shepherd for Right

Now Media that the original Hebrew Bible didn't have chapters and verses, so sometimes we can miss the interconnectedness of Scripture when we take it a verse at a time. The first Bible in English to use both chapters and verses was the Geneva Bible, published in 1560.[1] The church fathers added chapters and verses because Scripture was hard to read aloud, and these markers helped people locate which passage you were reading from. This was an excellent advancement for those of us who love sharing Scripture, but I also think it has caused us to think there are breaks in the text where the original writers didn't see breaks. I think these breaks can make us lose sight of the interconnectedness of God in stories of both suffering and salvation.

Remember, in the Old Testament or old covenant, you cannot separate the God of creation from God's covenantal promise to redeem that creation. He is the King who has made a promise to his people. And in the New Testament, Jesus, through the new covenant, keeps that promise with himself. I hope you can start making the same connection the ancient Israelites made. That every time you see chaotic waters, you are reminded of your Creator who still has power over them and who, through the passion of Christ, has redeemed us all.

First Corinthians 15:20–22 reads, "As it is, Christ has been raised from the dead, the firstfruits of those who have fallen asleep. For since death came through a man, the resurrection of the dead also comes through a man. For just as in Adam all die, so also in Christ all will be made alive" (csb).

After the crucifixion, the body of Jesus would also be laid in a garden, a clear signal back to the Adam of Genesis. The story doesn't end with you drowning. In heaven, we will all be singing. And because we have now segmented our Bible by adding chapters and verses that clearly mark for our minds promises about being a chosen people (1 Peter 2:9) or that we can ask for anything (John 16:24), we can start to get a bit inflated.

Little by little we start to confuse a God who wants us with a God who needs us. We replace a God who provided us righteousness with feelings of our own moral superiority. But then you grow up and you realize there are a lot of people God also wants, and they are pretty special too. It's hard to know for certain where you fit. Or how you fit. Or why you are even here.

God doesn't need me, I repeated this like a child who had just discovered that their whole life was a lie.

Sometimes I feel dumb when I pray. It feels like there are so many bigger and more important things for God to focus on than me and my problems. Sometimes I feel dumb because I don't know what to say. And sometimes I feel dumb because I do know what to say, but I am not sure I should be saying it. *Should I even be asking for this? Is this my vision or your vision? Am I supposed to give up or keep going? Did you put this on my heart or did I? Am I wrestling with you, or have I spent years wrestling with myself? God, I will go wherever you need me. But God, do you even need me?*

My prayers aren't always strong and faithful. Sometimes they are filled with uncertainty and weakness. And maybe those prayers are no less prayers. Maybe it's okay to look foolish to someone who is committed to you regardless. Maybe prayer is the safest space to bring ourselves as we are. Maybe it's one of the only places where we don't have to have "it" all figured out. Where the point isn't to tell God what you see but to ask him to reveal within you what he sees. What an honor it is to be fully exposed in prayer before someone who never needed me to impress them. Who gives me a place where I can fumble through clumsy desires. Where I can be uncertain and weak. Where it's not about right answers or even answers at all. God will always be God. Which means we are safe to be us.

In the morning, sober from my cry the night before, I started gathering my things to catch my flight. And that's when I discovered my shoes were gone. I had worn dressier shoes to the conference, but I always traveled in sandals that gave me arch support. They were pretty pricey for sandals. Pricey of course is relative, depending on how much money you have in your bank account, but for someone without savings at the time, I had to think twice before putting them in my Amazon cart. I searched all over the room, and they were nowhere to be found. Suddenly it hit me: Someone from housekeeping had been in my room and made the bed. Maybe their feet hurt and they saw those sandals. Maybe they had even less funds in their bank account than me but needed more arch support.

"I think the housekeeper stole my sandals," I said out loud into an empty room.

I thought for a second about calling the front desk. I am sure this case could be solved quickly. But then I thought none of it was a coincidence. Maybe God was revealing something to me about the world and my place in it. I had slept in many hotel rooms and never had anything stolen, much less something as basic as sandals. I had just cried the night before, feeling like I had nothing of value to offer God in comparison to all these other people I had seen. People more gifted, people more blessed, people who were serving the church in their passion and giftings. And I realized in that moment, as I put on dress shoes to wear with my sweatpants to walk through an airport, that it wasn't really about me at all, was it?

Your life is not about you as much as it's about other people. It is about people like the housekeeper who needed shoes. It is about people who have only a few dollars in their bank account and have to figure out how to trust God anyway. It is about people all over my town and university who may not get to go to the conference I went to or meet the leaders who inspired thousands, but may cross paths with me on campus.

I realized that morning after being the victim of petty theft that God doesn't just want *one* of us who is really special to do his will in this world. God wants *each* of us, who are all uniquely special, to collectively and individually do his will in this world. To leave millions of different footprints. Yes, there is always going to be someone more gifted and special than you. There is always going to be a better, cooler, more expensive pair of shoes. But that housekeeper didn't take my sandals because they were the best sandals in the hotel. Maybe they took them because they were the ones that were in the room they were assigned to clean. My shoes were the only ones that just so happened to be right there, next to their feet. God doesn't need you to be more special than everyone else. He needs you to be in the right room, at the right time, for the right person who needs support.

I never told the front desk. It was sandals, not a laptop, which had also been in my room available for the taking. It kind of felt like stealing a sandwich. Most people wouldn't do it unless they desperately needed it. Whoever had taken the sandals could keep them. What others do is between them and God. But what I had learned from it was between God and me.

Maybe God doesn't *need* us. But maybe he *wants* us to realize how much we *need* him. We need God to guide our footprints. To lead us to the right people. To worry more about being righteous than we do about being rich. And while I had been wondering where I fit, a stranger decided they needed my sandals. Not because they were special.

But because they were there.

"Again I tell you, it is easier for a camel to go through the eye of a needle than for a rich person to enter the kingdom of God."

Matthew 19:24 csb

DIVE DEEPER

1. How does comparison affect your focus?
2. Do you ever wonder where you fit? In what way?
3. What are some Bible verses that have been shared with you out of context?

CHAPTER 17

$212.40

$212.40. THAT IS HOW MUCH MONEY I HAD LEFT in my bank account on January 21, 2024. I recognize that this is a very intimate detail to casually drop. But it is important to me that I tell you the truth of where I was in my life financially. The reason I include this detail is that our finances can deeply impact how we see the rest of our lives. It's hard to feel the joy of the Lord before you when you are in financial duress. It is also hard to dream or think clearly or be hopeful. I won't bore you with the unexpected hits that slammed our bank account that Christmas. But by January 21, 2024, they had reached their full effect.

Studies are finding that more than 68 percent of US adults think today's children will be worse off than their parents.[1] Couple this with statistics that say it is getting harder in this world to climb financial obstacles. An *Economist* article found that in Britain "there is just a 9% chance of a child born in the bottom fifth of income distribution reaching the top fifth. In America, it is 7.5%."[2] America is still the land of opportunity, but if you aren't born into generational wealth, it is harder to attain it than one may realize. You have a 7 percent chance of radically reversing your status at birth, and that's not really odds many of us would bet on.

I had lunch with my friend Aundi Kolber, author of *Try Softer*, one day while sitting at a restaurant facing the harbor.

"I am feeling like I am supposed to do ministry full-time and quit my job," I told her. "It is a sense of urgency that is on my heart so heavy, and yet I don't know how that would ever be possible. I feel God prompting me to jump in headfirst, but I am too afraid to obey."

"Taking risks is a privilege," she said back to me with the care and compassion that only a trauma therapist could provide. "Risks aren't just about obedience. We also have to feel safe enough to take them."

Something about her saying that risk was often preceded by safety made me realize I wasn't being unfaithful. I was waiting. I was waiting for God to provide me with a sign of safety that would enable me to take this risk. Quitting your job to move full-time into your passion isn't something you do when you have only $212.40 in your bank account. And this wasn't me being disobedient. It was me wanting to be safe. Why was God putting things on my heart that didn't match with my reality? I was passionate, not delusional.

Around six months later I did an interview on *Viral Jesus* with a woman named Lana Silk, the chief executive officer of Transform Iran.[3] She seemed to be such a powerful woman of God. She talked about events in her life as if recounting the script of a movie. She would get a word from the Lord and get up and follow it, no questions asked. I asked her in that episode (which is still available if you want to hear her say it yourself) how she deciphers when God is calling her to something. I was trying to piece together my own life, but I pretended that I was asking for the enrichment of the audience.

She said two things in her response that I will never forget as long as I live. And one day in heaven, I intend to walk right up to her and tell her how many times these two points played in my mind as I tried to be faithful with my own journey. Her first point was that you cannot wait for God to move to be ready for the work God is calling you to. She said if you wait till God calls to get ready, it will be too late. She stressed the importance of a daily relationship with God, a daily strengthening of your spiritual muscles, so you can carry whatever task he asks you to hold. Discerning the voice of God doesn't start in big moments. It is a process of spiritual discernment you will navigate in hundreds of small moments. Walking out your purpose and calling is not something we start later; it's something we lean into right now. It will require you to walk out a million times with no pressure what you will eventually walk out when God has positioned you for this moment, and suddenly there is pressure.

It's the footprints we talked about and the just-keep-swimming metaphor we combed through. Living a life of passion will require you to get in the water. You can't train for the deep by sitting in a folding chair on the shore. Michael Phelps is the most decorated swimmer in history because he knew how to compete under pressure in the Olympics. Michael Phelps is often regarded as the greatest swimmer of all time, and even the greatest athlete of all time, because he kept getting in the water.

Michael Phelps reportedly swam thirteen kilometers a day, hitting roughly eighty thousand meters a week.[4] He trained every day, not even skipping practice on his birthdays. A *Forbes* interview has him saying he went five years without missing a single day of training, even if he was sick.[5] I think sometimes we look at people who are so clearly in their gifting and we wonder how they got there. It's like turning on the TV and seeing Michael Phelps win a gold medal but not seeing all the hours he had put into the sport without a camera crew around.

Lana Silk wanted people to know that she was living out her calling in a way that looked surreal because she had shown up to be with the Lord on days that looked very average. We don't wait for big moments to try to discern the voice of God. We live a daily life where we place ourselves before the Lord and ask for eyes to see and ears to hear. God doesn't just show up and call us to things. God journeys with us, step by step, day by day, little by little, to lives of reliance and surrender to his will for us. If you wait for a life-changing moment or opportunity to suddenly decide how to walk in the Spirit, it may be too late for the task that has just been opened.

The second thing she said I have repeated to people a dozen times since. She had a pastor once who told her that when discerning God's will in your life, she should look for at least two of these three Rs in a combination:

1. Romance
2. Reality
3. Revelation

She said *romance* was described for her as those moments when your heart just keeps feeling drawn toward that thing, whatever it is. Maybe it's quitting your job and going into your passion full-time. Maybe it's moving across the country. Maybe it's going back to school. Maybe it's starting a business. Maybe it's trying again in a romantic relationship after having had a bad experience. She said she pays attention to the desires of her heart and whether she feels romantic about the idea of moving forward toward that option.

Reality was described as what your actual reality looks like. For me, I was feeling this romantic pull toward full-time ministry, but I didn't see it in my reality. My reality was a bank account of $212.40. Maybe for you it is the opposite. Where the reality is there but the romance isn't. Someone has called you and offered you a job in a different state. That is the reality. But when you think about moving, the thought makes you feel overwhelmed and anxious, anything but romantic. Surely God couldn't be calling you to go across the country, could he?

Number three is *revelation*. This is where we get a direct supernatural revelation from God. Like when Abraham was called to leave the land of Ur. Or when Joseph had a dream where his brothers were bowing down to him. Or maybe God speaks to you through another person. God supernaturally reveals a plan for you or confirms something that you are experiencing either by romance (a heartfelt pull) or reality (a visible opportunity).

Lana said that these three Rs have helped her discern what God was calling her to. Of course, there may be a time when one R, like revelation, is enough to convince you—like God calling the prophet Jonah—but because the God I have experienced is kind, loving, and merciful, I would suggest that it is okay to ask God to confirm what he has revealed in either your romance or your reality so you can feel safe enough to move forward.

I've learned the tough lesson that there is a fine line between faith and delusion. I had learned that there was no golden scepter. No one is coming. So, when it came to going into ministry full-time, I felt my reality was looking pretty delusional, which is why I took a screenshot of my bank account at $212.40. I did not do it because I intended to tell you any of this. But subsequently I have felt that maybe it would bring you hope. I originally took that picture for me. I did it to remind myself of just how quickly a season can change. Just how abruptly the sun can come out. I did it so that I would never forget that tides can turn. The water can shift. The waves can break. And sometimes when you least expect it.

Isaiah 42:10 reads, "Sing to the LORD a new song, his praise from the ends of the earth, you who go down to the sea."

You can think you know exactly how your life is going to turn out, and in one unexpected moment, the Lord puts a new song in your mouth. Here is what I have learned in my journey that may be helpful to you in yours: This life may not go according to your plan. The reason for this is because our plans rarely account for darkness or discouragement or drowning. When we, who go down to the sea, are envisioning God's will for our lives, all we see is blissful waters. Our brains tend to pull the highlight reel. We see the good parts. We jump right to the destination with little understanding of just how much resistance we may face on our way to it. We skip the chaos.

In 1 Samuel 16:13, when Samuel told David he would be king, do you think David ever thought on that day that he would have to fight a giant? Run for his life? Hide in a cave? Or be a refugee until that plan was fulfilled? Esther became queen but was stunned when her uncle told her of Haman's plot to kill the Jews. I don't believe God plans the evils that may befall us in a broken world, but I know that he is actively redeeming, sustaining, and realigning us to our purpose despite the evil that may befall us in a broken world. Our plans rarely account for water heater bills, storms, or having $212.40 in our bank accounts.

But here is the good news about being in relationship with a heavenly being of limitless power and resources: God scans. God rescues. God sustains. God redeems. Though there be wind, though there be waves, though there be real agents of darkness and spiritual warfare, the promises of God will be kept. God is committed to you. He is the God of creation and the God of the covenant. God cannot be stopped.

This life may not look like you thought it would right now; our strategies rarely account for darkness. But I promise you,

God has a plan. You would be shocked at how quickly everything you think you know can change.

> "My sheep hear my voice, I know them, and they follow me. I give them eternal life, and they will never perish. No one will snatch them out of my hand."
>
> John 10:27–28 CSB

DIVE DEEPER

1. What in your life hasn't gone as planned?
2. Have you ever had a positive change that came about very suddenly?
3. Is there anything in your life you can apply the three Rs of *romance*, *reality*, and *revelation* to? Have you seen these in your past or present?

CHAPTER 18

JO

WHEN I WROTE *I'LL SEE YOU TOMORROW* WITH MY husband, Seth, I had high hopes that this would be the book that changed all my other books. But then, not a single influencer posted about it when it came out, despite the fifty people I had personally mailed it to. Seth and I recorded an interview for a podcast that had a pretty large audience. Then, after recording, the host sent an email to my publicist saying she wasn't going to air the interview. I had never had this happen before, and my publicist, Elizabeth, said she had never seen it done. The host said that they decided the episode would not run because "it wasn't a good fit." I was surprised. But also, not really. I often felt like I wasn't a good fit.

Our book never reached higher than five thousand on the Amazon sales charts the day it released. This is an early indicator that a book won't be hitting any bestseller lists. I felt like a failure by every possible metric. Writing had always been my greatest passion. The only thing I'd wanted to do since childhood. My precious instrument. And I was grappling with the reality that we had written a beautiful book that no one wanted to read. Just like my father with his television pilot that lost funding before it even got off the ground, *I'll See You Tomorrow* felt like the final weight that would make me sink. My team didn't even report to me first week's sales. You would avoid sharing these numbers only if you knew they would be demoralizing. I had to dig around and see what I could figure out through Amazon. What I discovered is that in the first week, we had sold only 511 copies through Amazon. To put this in perspective, my first book, *It's Not Your Turn*, did over five thousand copies in the first week. I had done 90 percent worse.

I am not sharing this with you because I want pity for my champagne problems. I am telling you this because I made a promise to the Lord when I was twenty-three years old.

"If you let me write books," I prayed so loud that all of heaven could hear me, "I will always be faithful in sharing with other people the truth of what we experience together. I will be honest about the pain, and I will testify to the praise. I will be transparent on what walking with the Lord looks like."

Of course, when I prayed this prayer at twenty-three, I had thoughts of mountaintops and grandeur. Deep water never entered the scenario. It never crossed my mind that I'd have $212.40, a book that sold 511 copies in its first week, or a podcast that I'd decide to cancel. No one makes promises like that if they know the undertow that lies ahead. I want to tell people about my successes, not my losses. I don't want to have a dad who doesn't know my name or a dream that slowly withers. I don't want to watch the sun shine on both the righteous and the wicked. But the last few years have left me with little else to report. And I had promised God that I'd tell the truth. He kept his end of the deal. He opened the door so I could write. So here we both are, transparent on these pages.

I had told the Lord I'd leave footprints that I hoped someone else might see their own path in. I am willing to show you my broken wings if it helps you feel less alone holding yours. This is faithfulness. Or trust. Probably both. What I didn't know when I made these vows, what I couldn't have known when I sat with my therapist asking her to tell me whether this Christian God had made me delusional, was that one of those 511 copies would be purchased by Jo.

I got a message from Jo on January 21, 2024, eleven days after I had written in my prayer journal, "God, don't you care if I drown?" Jo is a pseudonym I am using to protect the identity of a person with a golden scepter, someone God was in the process of sending to change my life.

Jo had, from time to time for the past year and a half, sent me a Venmo with a little encouraging message.

"God has a plan for you," she would say. And then send some money to make sure I knew she meant it. I always wrote her back and thanked her for encouraging me both financially and personally to keep going.

Here is a message she sent me on October 17, 2023, the same day I had put in my prayer journal, "God, don't you see me?" Later that morning I received a Venmo from Jo. It was in the amount of $1,000.

With it, she wrote the following message:

My dear sister, I know the timing is intentional, as there is literally no other way to explain how it all came into being. And
how you get put onto my heart at times. I just know God is
using you for great things and I'm thrilled he lets me be able to
help. You are so tiny but your voice is huge. It stands out!!! You
are bound to be tired with all you are giving and so many jobs.
*My prayer is that God will define his path for you in such a way,
and with such resources that you will only have one row to hoe.*

Jo was a total stranger. She had found me on the internet,
but unlike my friend Jamie, we had never met in real life. I
had never even seen an Instagram picture of her. She had no
idea that I had felt a deep pull by God to pursue my passion
full-time and quit a job I actually loved very much. "One row
to hoe" was exactly what I had been feeling God tell me I was
supposed to do. But I didn't know how it would be possible. She
also had no way of knowing that I had just been on a prayer
walk, crying to the Lord that it felt like he didn't see me.

My prayer is that God will define his path for you in such
a way and with such resources that you will only have one row
to hoe. How did Jo know what I was praying hundreds of miles
away in the dark? Her message gave me goosebumps. So much
so that I wrote it down in my prayer journal with the date. I
knew God had stirred her to encourage me. *Give me eyes to
see*, I prayed almost every day. I didn't know how this $1,000
connected to the larger scheme of going full-time into ministry,

but I had been tracking the hand of God long enough at this point to recognize it when he sends someone to encourage you to keep going, one more day.

I appreciated the Lord sending me the kindness of this stranger, although it didn't necessarily solve the problems in my real life. But I was moved that God wanted me to know he heard me. The Lord was near. I wouldn't drown. It felt worth recording in my journal. This is why I like to track God's hand in my life, so that when people say things I am praying in my secret space, I have dates to help me pay attention to how God may be encouraging me through his image bearers. This is why I want you to start doing this in your own life. Remember the track record. God delights in our delighting in him.

Throughout the next several months, Jo would periodically send another Venmo and another message. I appreciated it very much and always told her so. But on January 21, 2024, I was praying in my living room. I was about to make a professional pivot toward more corporate communication ventures. I would, of course, still do ministry. It was my passion. It was worthy of my suffering. But I also needed to make sure I could pay off my student loans and set money aside that my dad may eventually need. So, I was on my knees telling the Lord for the 900th time about my predicament just in case he hadn't heard me the other 899, when a Venmo came in from Jo.

"God is going to do something big for you in ministry," she wrote.

I sent her a message thanking her, then told her the truth. I decided to be transparent. I think I kind of felt bad that she was sending me money because she believed in my ministry, when I knew I was about to make a pivot. I was planning to sign a contract with a corporate speaking agent the very next day. I was spending time in prayer on Sunday, January 21, 2024, because something in my spirit felt hesitant to sign, but I didn't know if it was just that I was delusional. I decided to end my podcast after my incredible executive producer, Ed Gilbreath, needed to step back from his role for health reasons. The show wasn't growing anymore, and it felt like my sign that this was a necessary ending. But this also meant ending a significant portion of my income. I had to pivot.

I had only so much energy and I had $212.40. I was finally more stable than I had been in my twenties and it was time to fully commit to adulthood. Quit playing in the water. Get safety from the shore. I knew that this new door, though lucrative, would divide my energy. I didn't want to do that unless God was leading me into it. I love speaking, but what I love most about it is sharing my experiences with God and Scripture. God is my favorite conversation. I am quite possibly a fanatic. Corporate speaking was option C.

I was praying for God to reveal if this was the right path for me or if I was being unfaithful to my passion. I had never had an in-depth conversation with Jo, but because of the timing of her message, I assumed maybe God was sending me counsel. So, I did something that is very uncharacteristic of me when talking to strangers on the internet. I shared with her something very personal that no one outside of my immediate family knew. I told her I was so grateful for her encouragement, but the truth was, I was praying, at that exact moment actually, over a career pivot into corporate work.

"Did you ever google me, Heather?" she responded. She had given me her name a year ago and told me to look her up so I would know she was a real person. I had tried to look her up and didn't find anything. I also never knew which time would be the last time I would hear from her, so when nothing came up, I moved on.

For the first time, Jo revealed that her husband's family had a successful business and I could google it.

She provided me with the name of the business, and I started my Google search. There on my internet browser I discovered that Jo, the woman I had been receiving encouraging messages from for the last year and half—the same amount of time I had been navigating my own passion and discouragement, the same months that my friend Jamie had told me I was wintering, the same number of weeks I had told God I would drown—had recently sold her family business. The business was worth many millions of dollars. I had no idea that I had been messaging with a multimillionaire for a year and a half. I never asked her for a dime. I also didn't know she had so many. I never expected her to keep reaching out. I did, however, write down her words "one row to hoe" in my prayer journal and had prayed them nearly every day since she sent them.

That day we decided we should talk further.

A few days later we were on a video call. Jo told me that she couldn't explain it, but for the last year and a half, the Lord kept putting me on her heart. She had found my content online over a year before her husband sold his shares in their business. She had grown up in church but had stopped attending. She purchased *I'll See You Tomorrow* (she was one of the 511 people in that first week who did) and had connected with pieces of Seth's story as well as with mine. She had worked in communications for a government agency. She had a father who was a pastor who had passed away and was her spiritual hero. She loved the Lord and wanted to be faithful to him with what he had recently given her. What started with just social media morphed into reading my weekly newsletter and then became listening to my podcast (that I was now canceling). She even attended one of my live events I did in DC. She attended the event because it was only two hours from one of her homes. The only reason I was at that event, at that particular location, was because Beth Moore had invited me to speak with her, and that was the location she randomly gave me. For Beth it was probably a random invitation, but God had a plan, and as God does, he searches willing hearts who are open to his voice to bring it to fruition. Beth Moore has been and continues to be one of those willing hearts in my life. And because of her faithfulness to God, I met Jo. Jo started going back to church after that conference because of something I said in my message. I had told the audience, "Church is not a place we go, it is what we become in Christ. Biblically speaking, we are the church." Jo had needed my sandals. And I had been sitting in hotel rooms asking God if any of this mattered. Your life, your passion, your work, your faithfulness, always matter. You are a part of a much broader story. Even if you can't see it.

"I can't explain this to you because it doesn't make sense outside of God," Jo said to me on that video call. "But I am supposed to help provide the seed money so you can focus solely on ministry," she said. "This is what God has placed on my heart to do for you and for God."

My arms literally went numb. My mouth was incredibly thirsty. Vulnerability can cause your throat to get dry. It's a very common symptom of anxiety.

"Oh, and one more thing," Jo said with not the slightest clue at all how specifically powerful the next words out of her mouth would be for a little girl, who was now a woman, who had a dad who was dying of Alzheimer's. This woman, outside of a few Venmo messages, was a complete stranger to me. I had never discussed my dad's dreams or projects with her. I had never told her about the way I saw his heart break when he lost the funding for the last ministry project I ever saw him work on. It was an excellent concept, and then I watched God not bless it. It was a show. He had always felt God tell him he was supposed to create a show.

For over a decade, I thought those prayers my dad had prayed simply went unanswered. That they had expired. But then the Lord revealed something so powerful that it literally knocked the wind out of me.

"There is something I keep hearing from the Lord that I need to say out loud to you," Jo began offhandedly. "'It's a show!' 'It's a show!' I keep hearing this. I am not sure yet what it means. But I think I am also supposed to help you fund a show of some kind? The Lord will reveal our steps as we get closer.

But I want you to know I have more than enough resources to be a safety net for you, Heather. More than enough."

I hung up from the call and literally collapsed on the floor of my office. All my limbs went numb. I didn't know at all what was happening. But I did know that God remembered.

> "Every animal of the forest is mine, and the cattle on a thousand hills."
>
> Psalm 50:10

DIVE DEEPER

1. What is a pain or a praise you can share from your own life?
2. Is there someone God has pressed on your heart? Have you reached out to that person yet?
3. Does God still do miracles? Have you ever experienced one?

CHAPTER 19

WHAT DOES SWIMMING LOOK LIKE?

"I KEEP HAVING DREAMS THAT I AM DROWN-ing," I said to my non-Christian therapist.

"Are you drowning?" she asked me. She is very good at turning statements into questions.

"It feels like I am drowning," I said. I was gulping for air as we spoke.

"Heather, can I ask you something?" she asked, her tone of voice switching to curiosity.

"If you were watching someone swim, let's say the longest open-water swim ever done, what do you think the last few meters would look like to the person who was swimming it?"

The Guinness world record for the longest distance ocean swim is held by Pablo Fernandez of Spain in July 2021. He swam 250 kilometers or 155.34 miles.[1] I would hardly classify myself a Pablo Fernandez, but I could only assume that if I had swum 155 miles, that last stretch would look pretty hard.

"I bet it would look like death," I told her.

"It might even feel like you were drowning," she said back to me. "But to everyone else watching, it wouldn't. The last leg of any race or swim always feels like complete exhaustion. The person in it may feel like they are drowning, but to the people watching, it just looks like swimming." And then we sat in silence for so long that it started to get uncomfortable for the both of us.

I know what it feels like to be certain you can't do this for one more day. I know what it feels like to carry the weight of other people's prayers on your shoulders. I know what it feels like to jump headfirst into ice-cold water and not be sure if you are safe. I know what it feels like to swim for 155 miles and be certain that you'll drown.

But what if you aren't actually drowning? What if that is just part of long-distance swimming? What if there are seasons of life that were never meant for the shore? What if passion isn't passion until the sun has burned your wings? What if the only thing worse than falling is staying inside the maze?

We still have no idea what God will lead us to in this life. I am sure there is so much more failure ahead of both of us. I am not at all saying that now suddenly our lives make sense and God gives us a happy ending to all our desires. I am just telling you the truth of what I have seen. That no matter what happens next, we can trust God to hold us through it. We can trust him to go before us, and therefore we can hold more loosely to the plans we thought were crucial, that maybe won't come to fruition. Our plans rarely account for chaos. But God's plans always redeem. We don't have to have the answers. But we do have a God who feels like a safe space to bring all our questions.

There are prayers that have gone before you. And you have footsteps you can learn from. You know that the tide always changes. You know that the winter cannot last. You know how to trace the hand of God in the snow. You know how to mark the victories on stones that become the faith that you then stand on. And you know that even if all is shaken, the core of who you are in Christ will remain.

A month ago, my mom realized my dad didn't know who she was. They've been married over forty years. That's what Alzheimer's will do to a once perfectly happy family. It will make you forget that you were ever perfect or all that happy.

"I just know I love you," he told her when she asked him who she was.

When you don't know who God is anymore, when you don't know what your dreams are or what passion you are willing to keep suffering through, when you can't remember whether you are on option B or option 142, I hope those words are all that remain.

"Lord, I just know I love you."

When all is stripped away from us as bony Christians, may that be all that's true.

During my first year as a teacher, the chair of my department inspired my respect in his storytelling ability. I sat in on one of his lectures and I observed him draw in his students. They were hanging on his every word, thoroughly engaged. In contrast, at only twenty-four years old, nervous in front of thirty students, uncertain of my ability to convince them that I had the information they needed to learn, I did not feel the same sense of engagement in my classroom. After the lecture, I spoke with him. "I wish my students would be as attentive in my classroom as yours were," I admitted.

"I am seventy years old," he whispered, leaning toward me. "I have more stories than you do."

I need you to know your stories. I want you to write it all down. Pray for eyes to see and ears to hear. Don't just tell God what you don't see, ask God to reveal in you what he sees. I want you to be able to tell people your stories. Both the pain and the praise. Tell people the truth of what you have seen. Be transparent. Let your story encourage them in a season where it felt like no one would ever understand. Write down the dates and the prayers and the tears. Write down when it is awful, because it probably is. Tell them about the projects that got canceled and the funding that got pulled. Tell them about the lack of resources and the dead ends. My friend Gary says, "God loves to work in impossible and unlikely situations. It's so everyone knows it could only have been God."

My mentor José always told me, "You don't have to convince people with what you know. You just have to tell them what you've experienced."

Look for opportunities to make moments other people will remember. Pay attention to your own story and interrupt other people's lives with shock waves of kindness. Be the answer to other people's prayers. Be someone's Jo. Be the turning point on their page that no one ever saw coming. And trust me when I tell you that your entire life can change on a random Sunday afternoon. Every single one of us is always only one step or one hello or one day away from the season changing. Which is why you must endure.

The only way to have stories worth telling is to believe that your life is worth living. We have to be fully present in our own lives. Don't avoid deep water. Don't numb yourself from the cold. God will bring order out of chaos. Your job is to keep the passion burning in between. Life is what prepares you for life. The biggest mistake most adults will make is thinking that their story is over. Believing that life stops at forty or sixty or eighty. God loves impossible and improbable situations. It's one of the only ways you will know that it was only God.

I don't know what God is calling you to. But I do know that passion is calling. I believe with all my heart that God is calling you to serve right where you are. To stop resisting your own life. To put your feet in the water, even if the waves are starting to rise. And I believe you don't have to hustle harder to get doors to open. You just have to be faithful with what has been placed in your hands.

Isaiah 43:1–3 reads,

Now this is what the LORD says—the one who created you, Jacob, and the one who formed you, Israel—"Do not fear, for I have redeemed you; I have called you by your name; you are mine. When you pass through the waters, I will be with you, and the rivers will not overwhelm you. When you walk through the fire, you will not be scorched, and the flame will not burn you. For I am the LORD your God, the Holy One of Israel, and your Savior." (CSB)

I want you to multiply small moments. To be willing to walk the block with God. To be willing to serve your passions rather than have your passions be in service to you. To be willing to help the people next to you whether with a little or with a lot.

When the Roman poet Ovid wrote the story of Icarus, the wings that could bring freedom also came with a few instructions.

"Don't fly too low, and don't fly too high," Daedalus had said.

He was worried that if Icarus flew too low, the ocean would wet his feathers, and they might not recover. And if he flew too high, the heat of the sun would melt the wax, and the wings that carried him would disintegrate. We have learned something together, though, that I don't think Daedalus was ready to accept, but Icarus knew involuntarily. That life will always have seasons that bring you too low. You can't escape them. But ocean tides go in and out. Waves roll back to sea. The sun gives way to the darkness and the darkness gives way to the sun. Snow will turn to water. And to love and to suffer are both Christlike. To avoid either love or suffering would be to avoid life itself.

Start living your own life. Reengage in your own story. You think you are too old or too young or too forgotten or too unimportant for God to consume your life in passion? There is a fine line between faith and delusion. And it's hard to know which side you are on. Maybe you think it's too late for you. You gave up so much already and are sitting with what feels like so little. Your story doesn't feel like it is part of a broader one. It feels like no one is coming. All of those years you spent enduring, and you think you have nothing to show for it. But, my dear friend,

What if you're wrong?

The disciple, the one Jesus loved, said to Peter, "It is the Lord!" When Simon Peter heard that it was the Lord, he tied his outer clothing around him (for he had taken it off) and plunged into the sea.

John 21:7 CSB

DIVE DEEPER

1. Have you felt like it was too late for you and your passions? Do you still think that?
2. What may you be wrong about right now?
3. What is a story in this book that you will remember?
4. What is a line from this book you can share with someone to encourage them?

ACKNOWLEDGMENTS

TO MY HUSBAND, SETH DAY, THERE ARE NOT enough pages or enough books to ever communicate what you have been for me in my life. You are always the first thank-you.

To London, Hudson, and Sawyer, being your mom is my number one priority. I love you. And just keep swimming.

To Mom and Dad, all I have ever wanted to do is make you proud. Thank you for being unbelievably loving parents.

To my sister, Natasha, you are always my first reader. Thank you for telling me the truth. It's why I know I can always trust you.

To my brother, Joel, thank you for always showing me love, kindness, and hope.

To Caiden, there are so many prayers that have gone before you. I love watching you shine.

To Vickie, thank you for being my chosen family.

To Scarlett, just knowing you, and watching you, and reading your work has made me better.

ACKNOWLEDGMENTS

To Vimbo, I don't know how many prayers you have prayed over me throughout the years, but I know God heard every single one.

To Cortney, thank you for living your life with passion and exemplifying for me what it looks like to swim.

To Jo, you have transformed my life and my faith. Never beating the angel allegations.

To Nicole, Coty, Serena, and Terry, thank you for being not just Seth's family but my family.

To José Rojas, thank you for teaching me about deep water and to "stay humble and stay on my knees."

To my agent, Amanda Luedeke, thank you for believing in me all those years ago. I am so grateful for you.

To my editors, Kyle Olund, Lauren Bridges, and Jennifer McNeil, good books have good editors. And that is a fact. Thank you for being the best.

To my publisher, W Publishing, and Damon Reiss, thank you for believing in my work and making it available to the world.

To all our sources in this book, without your research and insights this book wouldn't exist. Thank you for bringing so much to the conversation.

PRAYER WALKS

I HAVE BEEN TAKING PRAYER WALKS FOR ABOUT eight years. Outside of reading through Scripture, I don't think there is another spiritual practice that has so deeply formed me. If you are wanting to try a prayer walk, (1) go to a safe walking area. Either a trail or a park or your neighborhood.

(2) Do not put in your headphones; this is time for just you and God without distractions. I don't have a set time when I do this. Sometimes it is only twelve minutes, other times I feel like I walked for days.

(3) Take your time to share with God transparently what you are wrestling through (out loud, not just in your head; let your own brain hear you).

(4) After I share with God what I see, I ask him to reveal within my heart what he sees. Pray for eyes to see and ears to hear. Make sure there is time where you are not talking. Make time to listen.

(5) I'd like to note here that if you can't hear the birds or the wind, which are external to you, you won't be able to hear a God who is speaking internally to you. You aren't listening for an external voice. You are listening for a still, small internal whisper. If you don't have good practice listening for that voice, start by trying to hear the birds and the wind.

(6) The name *Holy Spirit* means "comforter." The voice you hear will be comforting. I recommend doing this every day. But if you can't, aim for at least once a week when you Sabbath. It will change your perception of the Lord's closeness as you make time to pursue walks with God. The Lord is always near. Closer than you think.

(7) If you ever choose to do this exercise with another person, pray out loud over them. And then let them pray out loud over you. If you feel compelled to pray again a few minutes later, do so. There are no rules. Let the Spirit lead you.

NOTES

CHAPTER 1

1. James Orr, ed., *International Standard Bible Encyclopedia*, "Passion, Passions," Bible Study Tools, accessed October 14, 2024, https://www.biblestudytools.com/dictionary/passion-passions/.

CHAPTER 2

1. Glenn Paauw, "Waters of Chaos and Rivers of Life: The Bible's Story Told by Water," Institute for Bible Reading, November 25, 2019, https://instituteforbiblereading.org/bibles-story-told-by-water/.
2. Tim Mackie and Jon Collins, hosts, *BibleProject*, podcast, episode 21, "Chaotic Waters," June 25, 2018, https://bibleproject.com/podcast/series-h2r-p21-metaphor-e3-chaotic-waters/.
3. Amy L. Balogh, "Moses," in John D. Barry et al., eds., *The Lexham Bible Dictionary* (Lexham Press, 2016).

CHAPTER 4

1. *Oxford English Dictionary*, "passion," accessed October 14, 2024, https://www.oed.com/search/dictionary/?scope=Entries&q=passion.
2. Tim Mackie, "What's the Meaning of the Jewish Shema Prayer in the Bible?" BibleProject, May 26, 2017, https://bibleproject.com/

articles/what-is-the-shema/#:~:text=In%20other%20words%2C%20
the%20Shema,allegiance%20to%20any%20other%20gods.

CHAPTER 5

1. "Testament (in the Bible)," Encyclopedia.com, accessed
   August 15, 2024, https://www.encyclopedia.com/religion/
   encyclopedias-almanacs-transcripts-and-maps/testament-bible.

CHAPTER 6

1. Dictionary.com, "work," accessed October 14, 2024, https://www
   .dictionary.com/browse/work.

CHAPTER 7

1. Nadia Kounang, "What Is the Science Behind Fear?" CNN
   Health, October 29, 2015, https://www.cnn.com/2015/10/29/
   health/science-of-fear/index.html.
2. Mackie and Collins, "Chaotic Waters."

CHAPTER 8

1. Tim Mackie and Jon Collins, hosts, *BibleProject*, podcast, episode
   3, "Literary Styles," June 22, 2017, https://bibleproject.com/
   explore/video/literary-styles-bible/#:~:text=Tim%3A%20Well%20
   first%20and%20foremost,up%20the%20remaining%2024%20
   percent.
2. Heather Day, "Use of Stories in Courses and Student
   Engagement at Southwestern Michigan College," (PhD diss.,
   Andrews University, 2018), https://digitalcommons.andrews.
   edu/dissertations/1661/.

CHAPTER 9

1. J. R. Moehringer, "How Travis Kelce Manifested the Best Year of
   His Life," *Wall Street Journal*, November 20, 2023, https://www.wsj
   .com/style/travis-kelce-chiefs-taylor-swift-relationship-413ce0d7.
2. Linda Grant, "Ruth Bader Ginsburg and Harvard
   Law: A 64-Year Journey," *Harvard Law Bulletin*,
   September 23, 2020, https://hls.harvard.edu/today/
   ruth-bader-ginsburg-and-harvard-law-a-sixty-four-year-journey/.

CHAPTER 10

1. Lindsay Terry, "Story Behind the Song: 'Midnight Cry,'" *St. Augustine Record*, August 11, 2016, https://www.staugustine.com/story/lifestyle/faith/2016/08/12/story-behind-song-midnight-cry/16300477007/.
2. "Jim Carrey Reveals His Father's Failure Inspired His Comedic Dreams," ABC News, May 27, 2014, https://abcnews.go.com/Entertainment/jim-carrey-reveals-fathers-failure-inspired-comedic-dreams/story?id=23882862.

CHAPTER 11

1. "K. A. Ellis: Loving the Widow," posted June 29, 2019, by The Gospel Coalition, YouTube, https://www.youtube.com/watch?si=g791begJnK53vVF2&v=zqywDp2XDfQ&feature=youtu.be.
2. Kenneth E. Bailey, *Jesus Through Middle Eastern Eyes: Cultural Studies in the Gospels* (IVP Academic, 2008), chapter 15.
3. Rabbi Shaya Karlinsky, "Chapter 1: Mishna 5: Part 2," Torah.org, November 4, 2015, https://torah.org/learning/maharal-p1m5part2/.

CHAPTER 12

1. 1 Kings 19:19; 1 Kings 17:7–16; John 4.

CHAPTER 13

1. Idina Menzel, "Let It Go," *Frozen Original Motion Picture Soundtrack*, Walt Disney Records, 2013, https://open.spotify.com/track/0qcr5FMsEO85NAQjrlDRKo.

CHAPTER 14

1. Peter Enns, *The Sin of Certainty* (HarperCollins, 2017).

CHAPTER 15

1. Katherine May, *Wintering: The Power of Rest and Retreat in Difficult Times* (Riverhead Books, 2020).

CHAPTER 16

1. "The Geneva Bible: The First English Study Bible," Dunham Bible Museum, accessed October 14, 2024, https://hc.edu/museums/dunham-bible-museum/tour-of-the-museum/past-exhibits/from-geneva-the-first-english-study-bible/.

CHAPTER 17

1. Michelle Fox, "A Majority of Americans Think Children Will Be Financially Worse Off Than Their Parents, Survey Finds," CNBC, July 21, 2021, https://www.cnbc.com/2021/07/21/many-americans-think-children-will-be-financially-worse-off-than-their-parents.html.

2. "It's Becoming Harder to Get Rich If You're Born Poor," *Economist*, November 25, 2021, https://www.economist.com/films/2021/11/25/its-becoming-harder-to-get-rich-if-youre-born-poor.

3. Heather Thompson Day, host, *Viral Jesus*, podcast, episode 112, "Lana Silk: An Iranian Daughter's Mission," *Christianity Today*, February 29, 2024, https://www.christianitytoday.com/ct/podcasts/viral-jesus/lana-silk-iranian-daughters-mission.html.

4. Sebastian Mikkelsen, "Michael Phelps: The Training Regimen of the Most Decorated Swimmer in Olympic History," Olympics.com, June 5, 2023, https://olympics.com/en/news/michael-phelps-training-regimen-workut-diet.

5. "Michael Phelps: Going Five Years Without Missing a Single Day of Training," *Forbes*, October 24, 2016, https://www.forbes.com/video/5180394324001/michael-phelps-going-five-years-without-missing-a-single-day-of-training/.

CHAPTER 19

1. "Longest Distance Ocean Swim (Marathon Swimming)," Guinness World Records, accessed October 14, 2024, https://www.guinnessworldrecords.com/world-records/longest-ocean-swim#:~:text=The%20longest%20distance%20ocean%20swim,on%2019%2D20%20July%202021.

ABOUT THE AUTHOR

DR. HEATHER THOMPSON DAY IS AN INTER-denominational speaker and an ECPA bestseller and has been a contributor for Religion News Service, *Christianity Today*, *Newsweek*, and the Barna Group.

Heather was a communications professor for nearly fifteen years, teaching both graduate and undergraduate students in public speaking, persuasion, and social media. She is now the founder of It Is Day Ministries, a nonprofit organization that trains churches, leaders, and laypeople in what Heather calls "Cross Communication," a gospel-centered communication approach that points you higher, to the cross, every time you open your mouth.

Heather's writing has been featured on outlets like the *Today Show* and the National Communication Association. She has been interviewed by BBC Radio Live and *The Wall Street Journal*.

She believes her calling is to stand in the gaps of our churches. She is the author of nine books, including *It's Not Your Turn* and *I'll See You Tomorrow*.

You can learn more by going to HeatherThompsonDay .com.